SPECTRUM

Writing

Grade 8

Published by
Frank Schaffer Publications®

Frank Schaffer Publications®

Spectrum is an imprint of Frank Schaffer Publications.

Send all inquiries to:
Frank Schaffer Publications
8720 Orion Place
Columbus, Ohio 43240-2111

Spectrum Writing—grade 8

ISBN 0-7696-5288-3

3 4 5 6 POH 11 10 09 08 07

Table of Contents Grade 8

Chapter 1 Writing Basics

Chapter 2 Expressive Writing

Chapter 3 Descriptive Writing

Chapter 4 Writing to Entertain

Table of Contents, continued

Chapter 5 Persuasive Writing

Chapter 6 Explanatory Writing

Chapter 7 Informational Writing

Chapter I
Lesson 1 Staying on Topic

In a picture, the details normally fit the main idea. In a paragraph, all of the details should also fit the main idea. That's another way of saying that each sentence must stay on topic.

The following paragraph contains a sentence that is not on topic. Read the paragraph, and underline the topic sentence. Then, draw a line through the sentence that does not support the topic sentence.

> I think city life is great. I know all my neighbors in the apartment building, and they know me. I walk only a block to get to school. All the things we need, such as a grocery store, the bank, the library, and the train station, are within easy walking distance. We usually ride the 9:15 express when we go across town to visit my grandma. I can't imagine living anywhere else.

List two details from the paragraph above that support the main idea.

_____

_____

Now, write your own paragraph about city, suburban, or country life. Remember to stay on topic. Stick to one main idea, and make sure that all of your detail sentences support that main idea. When you are finished, underline your topic sentence.

_____

_____

_____

_____

_____

_____

_____

_____

_____

_____

_____

_____

_____

Lesson 2 The Writing Process

Writers follow a plan when they write. The steps they take make up the writing process. Following these five steps leads to better writing.

Step 1: Prewrite

Think of prewriting as the "getting your act together" stage. Writers might choose a topic, or they might list everything they know about a topic already chosen. They might conduct research and take notes. Then, writers may organize their ideas by making a chart or diagram.

Step 2: Draft

Writers put their ideas on paper. This first draft should contain sentences and paragraphs. Good writers keep their prewriting ideas nearby. There will be mistakes in this draft, but there is time to fix them later.

Step 3: Revise

Writers change or fix their first draft. They move ideas around, put them in a different order, or add information. They make sure they used clear words and that the sentences sound good together. This is also the time to take out ideas that are not on topic.

Step 4: Proofread

Writers usually write or type a neat, new copy. Then, they look again to make sure everything is correct. They look especially for errors in capitalization, punctuation, and spelling.

Step 5: Publish

Finally, writers make a final copy that has no mistakes. They are now ready to share their writing. That might mean turning in an assignment, sending a letter, or posting your work on a bulletin board for others to read.

Lesson 2 The Writing Process

What does the writing process look like? Abby used the writing process to write a paragraph about her next-door neighbor. Her writing steps below are out of order. Label each step with a number and the name of the step.

Step ____: _____

     My neighbor, Mrs. Garcia, lives in 4D, and she just loves people. Her children are all grown up now, but Mrs. Garcia is never happier than when they come to see her. She always says that the more people she has in her apartment, the happier she is. Mrs. Garcia also loves to cook. She often offers to share some stew or homemade bread. I think the food just gives her an excuse to be around people.

Step ____: _____

     My neighbor is Mrs. Garcia. She lives in 4D. She just loves people. her children are all grown up now, but Mrs. Garcia is never happier than when they come to see her She always says that the more people she has in her apartment, the happier she is. Mrs. Garcia also cooks. She often offers to share. I think the food just give her an excuse to be around us.

Step ____: _____

My neighbor, Mrs. Garcia lives in 4D, and she just loves people. her children are all grown up now, but Mrs. Garcia is never happier than when they come to see her. She always says that the more people she has in her apartment, the happier she is. Mrs. Garcia also loves to cook. She often offers to share some stew or homemade bread. I think the food just give her an excuse to be around people.

Step ____: _____

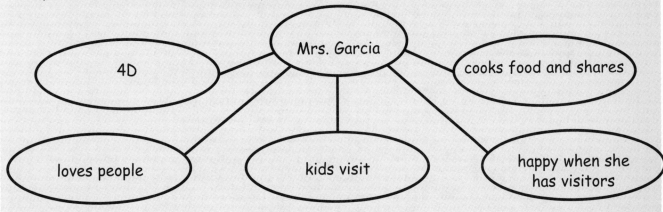

Step ____: _____

     My neighbor is Mrs. Garcia. She lives in 4D. She just loves people. her children are all grown up now, but Mrs. Garcia is never happier than when they come to see her She always says that the more people she has in her apartment, the happier she is. Mrs. Garcia also cooks. She often offers to share. I think the food just give her an excuse to be around us.

Lesson 3 Audience

Imagine that you are in an Introduction to Technology class. The teacher stands up and says this:

> PC CPU input/output transits via bus systems to peripheral devices.

The teacher has forgotten to think about her audience. Her statement doesn't belong in an introductory course. It would be better suited for experienced computer technicians.

Here is the statement she should have made to her eighth-grade students in an introductory class:

> In a personal computer, information and instructions go between the central processing unit and components, such as a hard disk or a CD reader, by means of internal cables.

Speakers and writers both must think about their audience. If they do not, they will not communicate effectively.

> Writers need to consider these questions every time they write:
>
> What will my audience enjoy?
>
> What are they interested in?
>
> What will make them want to keep on reading?
>
> What do they already know?
>
> What will they understand?

Here is part of an article from the foods section of a newspaper. Anyone who picks up the paper might read this article.

> Shirring is an old-fashioned technique for preparing eggs. Shirred eggs are perfect with a little salt and pepper for those who like things simple. Others prefer a few breadcrumbs, grated cheese, or chopped herbs sprinkled over their shirred eggs.

What did the writer fail to provide for his audience?

_____

_____

Lesson 3 Audience

Imagine the local school principals want everyone in the whole school district to participate in a School Spirit Day. Everyone is supposed to wear school colors, and some prizes will be given for outfits that show the most spirit. Write a memo that first-grade teachers read out loud so their students can understand what School Spirit Day is all about. Remember to ask yourself the five questions on page 8 before you write.

_____
_____
_____
_____
_____
_____
_____
_____
_____

Now, write another version of the memo that will go to the high school students. What will they want or need to know that is different from what the first-graders needed to know?

_____
_____
_____
_____
_____
_____
_____
_____
_____

Lesson 4 Write a Paragraph

Here is what you know about paragraphs.

- A paragraph is a group of sentences about the same topic.
- The first line of a paragraph is indented.
- The main idea of a paragraph is what the paragraph is all about.
- A paragraph's main idea is usually stated in a topic sentence.
- The topic sentence may fall anywhere in the paragraph.
- Each sentence in a paragraph supports the topic.
- The sentences appeal to the audience.

What is your idea of a great movie? List some details that would be part of your perfect movie.

Details:

_____   _____

_____   _____

_____   _____

Review your list. Think about the order in which you want to present your details in a paragraph. If you wish, number them. Then, use the lines on this page to draft a paragraph about your idea for a great movie.

_____

_____

_____

_____

_____

_____

_____

_____

_____

_____

_____

_____

Lesson 4 Write a Paragraph

Read through your paragraph. Ask yourself these questions. If necessary, make changes to your paragraph.

Questions to Ask About a Paragraph
Is the first line indented? **Does the topic sentence express the main idea?** **Does each sentence support the topic sentence?** **Does each sentence express a complete thought?** **Are the ideas in the paragraph appropriate for the audience?**

Now that you have thought about the content, or meaning, of your paragraph, proofread it for errors. Look through several times, looking for a certain kind of error each time. Use this checklist.

____ spelling   ____ end marks

____ capitalization   ____ punctuation

Now, rewrite your paragraph. Use your neatest handwriting and make sure there are no errors in the final copy.

_____

_____

_____

_____

_____

_____

_____

_____

_____

_____

_____

_____

_____

_____

A personal narrative is a true story an author writes about his or her own experiences. A personal narrative doesn't have to be about the time you rescued nine people from a burning building or the day you amazed your preschool teacher by reciting the entire *Declaration of Independence*. Personal narratives can be about ordinary things that happen to ordinary people. Read Marlon's personal narrative.

Dog Day

The sign on the bulletin board at the library said that anyone could participate. More importantly, it said that any dog could participate. You didn't have to have a fancy dog that had bows in its hair. You didn't have to have a dog with three names. Anyone could have any dog.

I am anyone, and I have a dog. My dog's name is Pierre. No, he's not a poodle. He has a fancy French name because he tipped over a bucket of paint and then walked through the mess when he was a puppy. After a big chase scene and a little too much excitement, Mom said he was "a regular Renoir." So, we gave him Renoir's first name.

Pierre is a good dog, but he isn't what you would call "trained." He sits, sometimes. He lies down, but only when I get down on the floor with him. He almost always comes when I call him, though. As it turns out, that is his most important skill.

Pierre and I went to the First Annual Community Dog Show on a cool Saturday morning in May. There were tons of other people and dogs there. Some were dressed up in costumes—the people and their dogs. Some people, however, had regular clothes on. There were so many colors and noises that I almost felt dizzy.

I found the registration table and stuck the end of Pierre's leash into my pants pocket. While I was busy signing in, I felt a tug at my hip. By the time I looked down, the leash was gone and Pierre had taken off across the grounds. In three seconds, I saw three other dogs break loose and tear off after Pierre. I was right behind them, dodging through the crowd as fast as I could.

Pierre and his followers headed for the show ring. They ran right under the temporary fence. Even in my panic, it struck me that it looked just like racers crossing a finish line. This race was just beginning, though. The dogs in the show ring dashed away from their surprised owners and joined in. Twice around the ring they went, and the crowd watched while a few owners tried crazily to chase and grab their dogs. It was turning into a comedy when Pierre led the whole parade out of the ring and toward the edge of the park...and a very busy street.

Lesson 1 Personal Narrative

When I saw what was happening, I finally found my voice. "Pierre! Come!" I shouted through my cupped hands. The herd of dogs turned in a graceful arc, like a comet with its fiery tail streaming out behind, as Pierre responded to my call. At last, he came to rest at my feet, tongue lolling.

All around me, dog owners were grabbing up trailing leashes. I suddenly realized that my knees were shaking. I sat down next to Pierre and praised and scolded and hugged him all at the same time. A woman and her panting dog came over to me. She stuck out her hand and said, "It's a good thing your dog is so well trained." I shook her hand limply and kind of nodded. Was she kidding me? Then, a man passed by and patted me on the shoulder. "Good job, young man."

I had expected to get kicked out, but the dog show went on, and they let Pierre and me into the ring. We got a green participation ribbon, which was fine. I was just glad to be there. At the end of the day, I was awfully glad to go home again, tightly gripping the leash of my well-trained dog, Pierre.

NAME _____

Lesson 1 Personal Narrative

> Here are the features of a personal narrative:
>
> - It tells a story about something that happens in a writer's life.
> - It is written in the first person, using words such as *I, me, mine,* and *my.*
> - It uses time and time-order words to tell events in a sequence.
> - It expresses the writer's personal feelings.

Some people write personal narratives because they want to share their thoughts and feelings. Some write because they want to entertain their readers. Others might want to do both. As always, writers of personal narratives keep their audience in mind. What do they want to share with those readers?

So, what could you write a personal narrative about? Here are some idea-starters.

your first pet   the noisiest place you've been
an exciting event   an embarrassing moment
how you overcame a fear   the weirdest thing you ever saw
a rainy day

What memories came to mind as you read these idea-starters? Jot some notes about those memories here. One of these could be the start of a great personal narrative!

Idea-starter: _____

_____

Idea-starter: _____

_____

Idea-starter: _____

_____

Idea-starter: _____

_____

Lesson 2 Sequence of Events

On a dark and stormy night,...

This phrase has become unoriginal because it has been used so much. At the same time, writers of personal narratives need to tell when things happen and in what order. Sometimes, events do happen on a dark and stormy night.

Reading about events in order helps readers understand what happens and why. Think of some time-order words or phrases. List them below. The list is started for you.

| tonight | after dark | at bedtime |
| Friday | last night | midnight |

_____ _____ _____

_____ _____ _____

_____ _____ _____

_____ _____ _____

Now, use some of the time-order words you listed. Write a sentence that could be from a personal narrative. Use a time-order word or phrase at the beginning of your sentence.

_____

_____

_____

Write a sentence about something you did last week. Use a time-order word or phrase in the middle or at the end of your sentence.

_____

_____

_____

Think about a dark and stormy night. What is happening? Write a sentence about it without using the phrase "on a dark and stormy night."

_____

_____

_____

Lesson 2 Sequence of Events

In addition to time-order words, transition words help readers know when things happen and in what order. Here are some common transition words.

also	as soon as	because	but	finally
meanwhile	next	so	soon	therefore when

Here is a paragraph from Marlon's personal narrative on pages 12 and 13. Circle the transition words when you find them.

> When I saw what was happening, I finally found my voice. "Pierre! Come!" I shouted through my cupped hands. The herd of dogs turned in a graceful arc, like a comet with its fiery tail streaming out behind, as Pierre responded to my call. At last, he came to rest at my feet, tongue lolling.

Think about a time when you did something in public. Where were you? What happened? What did you think about? Write the sequence of events in a paragraph. Remember that it is important to use time-order words, but don't start every sentence with a transition word. Use different sentence styles to keep your writing interesting.

_____

_____

_____

_____

_____

_____

_____

_____

_____

_____

_____

_____

_____

_____

_____

Lesson 3 Active Voice

Usually, the subject of a sentence does the action. That is easy to see in this sentence:

> The pitcher threw the ball.

The verb in the sentence is an **active verb** because the subject, *pitcher*, did the action, *threw*.

What about this sentence?

> The ball was thrown.

Ball is the subject of the sentence. Does the ball do the action? No, the ball does not do the action. The ball "receives" the action. The verb, *was thrown*, is a **passive verb** because the subject does not do the action.

Passive verbs are always two-part verbs. One of these helping verbs—*am, is, was, be, been*—always works with a main verb. That does not mean that whenever you see one of those helping verbs, you are looking at a passive verb, however.

> Passive verb: The pitch *was missed.*

> Active verb: The batter *was missing.*

How can you tell the difference? Ask yourself these two questions:

> What is the subject?

> Is the subject doing the action?

If the answer to the second question is "no," then you have a passive verb.

Sometimes, writers have to use passive verbs when they write. Maybe the writer doesn't know who did the action, so, "The ball was thrown" is the only option. Most of the time, however, writing is clearer and more interesting if writers use active verbs.

Lesson 3 Active Voice

Compare these two paragraphs. The one on the left is written mostly with passive verbs. The one on the right is written with active verbs. What do you notice?

The Maine Lions were defeated in a close game with the Marathon Warriors here on Sunday afternoon. The Lions were shut down by the Warriors with a 3–2 score. Maine's batters were bested by the Marathon pitchers, who seemed at the top of their game. Maine's top pitchers were plagued with injuries. The first run was scored by Marathon's fielder Wendell in the second inning. The second and third runs were scored in the third inning by Hunley and Cruz. Maine's two runs were scored in the ninth inning by Hector and Clary.

The Marathon Warriors defeated the Maine Lions in a close game here on Sunday afternoon. The Warriors shut down the Lions with a 3–2 score. The Marathon pitchers, who seemed at the top of their game, bested Maine's batters. Injuries plagued Maine's top pitchers. Marathon's fielder Wendell scored the first run in the second inning. In the third inning, Hunley and Cruz scored the second and third runs. Maine's Hector and Clary scored two runs in the ninth inning.

Underline the subject of each sentence below. Put an **X** next to each sentence that contains a passive verb.

_____ Andy Hunley hit a home run.

_____ The crowd was cheering.

_____ The last run was scored by Gabe Cruz.

_____ The game was won by the Warriors.

Practice writing sentences with active verbs. First, look at the sentences above that have passive verbs. Rewrite one of those sentences with an active verb.

_____

_____

Now, write a new sentence about a baseball game or other sport. Use an active verb.

_____

_____

Lesson 4 The Writing Process: Personal Narrative

A personal narrative can be about anything that the writer actually experienced. If you have survived a month in the wilderness, that would be a great topic. But if you haven't, there are lots of other things to write about. Remember the narrative you read on pages 12 and 13? Marlon wrote about his dog. It was a little exciting, but nothing dangerous or life threatening happened. It was just an event that caused Marlon to think a little bit. Follow the writing process to develop a personal narrative about a normal event in your own life. How did it change you?

Prewrite

Look again at the idea-starters on page 14 and the notes you made. Choose one of those ideas, or another idea that you like and begin to explore it here.

My idea: _____

Use this idea web to collect and record details. Write down as many as you can.

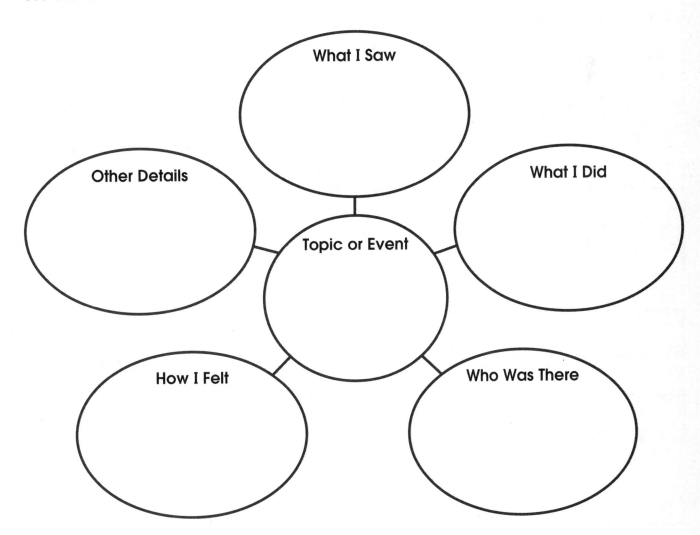

Lesson 4 The Writing Process: Personal Narrative

Now, it is time to put your ideas in order. Think about the "story" you are about to tell in your personal narrative. Use the sequence chart on this page to list the events in order. Don't worry about details here, just put the events in order.

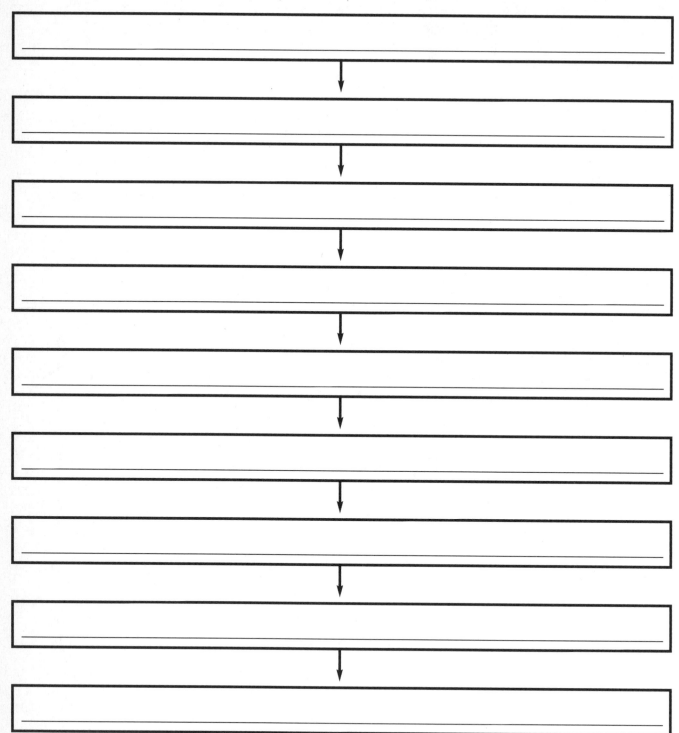

Lesson 4 The Writing Process: Personal Narrative

So far, you have chosen a topic, collected ideas, and put them in order. Now, focus on some sensory details. They will make your readers feel as if they are right there with you, experiencing whatever event you write about.

In the boxes below, record sensory details about each part of the narrative you are planning. Remember to be very specific. If you are writing about an amusement park and you want to tell how the roller coaster looked, don't just say it was colorful, or that it had lights on it. Maybe the tracks were "lined with white lights." Or maybe the roller cars "sparkled and flashed with red and blue lights."

What My Readers Should See

What My Readers Should Hear

What My Readers Should Smell

What My Readers Should Feel

What My Readers Should Taste

Lesson 4 The Writing Process: Personal Narrative

Draft

Write a first draft of your personal narrative on this page. Continue on another sheet of paper if you need to. Look back at your sequence chart and at the sensory details you recorded to help keep your ideas in order. As you write, don't worry about getting every word just right. Write your ideas in sentences and put the events in order.

_____

_____

_____

_____

_____

_____

_____

_____

_____

_____

_____

_____

_____

_____

_____

_____

_____

_____

Write an idea for a title here.

Title:_____

Lesson 4 The Writing Process: Personal Narrative

Revise

One of the hardest things for any writer to do is to "fix" or change his or her own work. However, even experienced, professional writers know that they can almost always improve their first drafts. Improve your own first draft by answering the questions below. If you answer "no" to any questions, those are the areas that might need improvement. Make notes on your draft about changes you might make.

> - Did you tell about just one event or one "thing" in your narrative?
>
> - Did you tell events in order? Did you use time and time-order words to show when events happened?
>
> - Did you include sensory details to make readers feel as if they are right there with you?
>
> - Did you tell how you felt about the events? Do readers get a sense of your personal feelings?
>
> - Did you use active verbs?
>
> - Read your work out loud. Do your sentences flow well?

Now, focus on making sure you included details that will keep your readers interested. Did you use specific descriptive words, vivid verbs, and precise nouns?

When Marlon revised his personal narrative, he added some descriptive words and phrases. Here is how Marlon changed his closing paragraph.

I had expected to get kicked out, but the dog show went on, and they let Pierre and me into the ring. We got a green participation ribbon, which was fine. I was just glad to be there. At the end of the day, I was awfully glad to go home again with tightly gripping the leash of my well-trained dog Pierre.

Lesson 4 The Writing Process: Personal Narrative

Write the revision of your first draft. As you revise, remember to keep readers interested by using vivid descriptive words.

_____

_____

_____

_____

_____

_____

_____

_____

_____

_____

_____

_____

_____

_____

_____

_____

_____

_____

_____

_____

_____

_____

Now that you have revised your draft, are you still happy with your title? If not, write a new title here.

Title:_____

Lesson 4 The Writing Process: Personal Narrative

Proofread

Now, it is time to correct those last errors. As you proofread, read for just one kind of error at a time. Read through once for capital letters, once for end punctuation, and once for spelling. Here is a checklist to help you proofread your revised narrative.

____ Each sentence begins with a capital letter.

____ Each sentence ends with the correct punctuation (period, question mark, or exclamation point).

____ Each sentence states a complete thought.

____ All words are spelled correctly.

When proofreaders work, they use certain symbols. Using these symbols makes their job easier. They will make your job easier, too.

Use these symbols as you proofread your personal narrative. Also, read your writing out loud. You might catch a mistake that you overlooked before. Proofread carefully!

- C̲ capitalize this letter.
- Add a missing end mark: ⊙ ? !
- Add a comma‸please.
- Fix incoʳrect or misspelled words.
- "Use quotation marks correctly," she reminded.
- ~~Delete~~ this word.
- Lowercase this L̸etter.

Publish

Write or type a final copy of your personal narrative on a separate sheet of paper. If you wish, mount a photo to display with your narrative. Double-check one last time for errors.

Chapter 3
Lesson 1 Sensory Details

> The new restaurant in the century-old Capital City Hotel is open for business, and it is well worth the trip. While you wait for a table, the colorful fish in the wall-sized aquarium will entertain you. Once you step into the dining room, you will feel as though you have stepped back in time. The gleaming, golden oak tables and chairs, and the red-flocked wallpaper will pull you back to the stately hotel's earliest days. Once seated, guard against smacking your lips at the perfectly prepared meats, interestingly seasoned potatoes, and crisp-tender fresh vegetables.

In a description, a writer's goal is to help readers see, hear, smell, feel, or taste what is being described. Writers use **sensory details**, or details that appeal to readers' senses, in their description. For example, in the paragraph above, "red-flocked wallpaper" helps you see and feel the walls. What other sensory details does the paragraph contain? List them here according to whether the detail helps you see, hear, smell, feel, or taste what is being described. Some details might fit into more than one category.

See: _____ _____ _____

Hear: _____ _____ _____

Smell: _____ _____ _____

Feel: _____ _____ _____

Taste: _____ _____ _____

The room you are in right now probably does not have red-flocked wallpaper. What kind of walls does it have? Gleaming white? Dull tan? Cluttered? Empty? Write some sensory details about the room in which you are sitting.

See: _____ _____ _____

Hear: _____ _____ _____

Smell: _____ _____ _____

Feel: _____ _____ _____

Taste: _____ _____ _____

NAME _____

Lesson 1 Sensory Details

Think of a restaurant in which you have eaten. Was it a "fine dining experience," or were you in a fast-food chain? Imagine yourself in the restaurant. Can you describe the experience so that a reader feels as if he or she is right there?

First, write the sights, sounds, smells, textures, and flavors you experienced.

Sights:_____ _____ _____

Sounds: _____ _____ _____

Smells: _____ _____ _____

Textures: _____ _____ _____

Flavors: _____ _____ _____

Now, put your words to work. Describe what it was like to be in this restaurant. Appeal to all five of your readers' senses.

_____

_____

_____

_____

_____

_____

_____

_____

_____

_____

_____

_____

_____

_____

_____

_____

_____

_____

Lesson 2 Adjectives and Adverbs

A complete sentence requires one noun or pronoun and one verb.

> We sing.

Adjectives and adverbs describe, or modify, the words in a sentence to add interest or detail.

Adjectives modify nouns or pronouns. They tell *what kind, how much* or *how many*, and *which ones*.

Adverbs modify verbs, adjectives, or another adverb. They tell *how, when, where*, or *to what degree*. Many adverbs end in *ly*, but some do not, such as *not, never, very*, and *always*.

Adjectives at Work

This sentence contains no adjectives.

> The choir sings at the concert.

What kind of choir is it? It is a middle-school choir.

How many choir members are there? There are 30 of them.

What kind of concert is it? It is a benefit concert.

Here is the new sentence. Notice that the adjectives go right before the nouns that they describe. This is almost always true. Think about all the information in this sentence compared with the original sentence.

> The 30-member middle-school choir sings at the benefit concert.

Read the sentences below. Think of at least two adjectives to add to them. Then, write the new sentence. Remember, an adjective tells more about a noun or pronoun.

One singer performed a solo.

_____

The girls wore dresses.

_____

The boys wore pants and shirts.

_____

The director bowed to the audience.

_____

Lesson 2 Adjectives and Adverbs

Adverbs at Work

Start with the same basic sentence and see how some adverbs liven it up.

> The choir sings in the concert

How does the choir sing? The choir sings enthusiastically.

When does the choir sing? The choir sings first.

Here is our new sentence. Notice that one adverb comes right before the verb it describes. The other falls right after the verb.

> The choir enthusiastically sings first in the concert.

Look at each sentence below. Add information about *how, when, where,* or *to what degree* with an adverb. Write your new sentence on the line.

One singer performed a solo.

_____

He dropped the microphone.

_____

The judges clapped and nodded their heads.

_____

Look at how both adjectives and adverbs work in this sentence.

>   final expertly lovely
> The soloist sang a ballad.

Improve each sentence by adding one adjective and one adverb to make the sentences more vivid.

The audience stood and clapped for the soloist.

_____

The soloist's mother wiped tears from her eyes.

_____

The singer left the stage.

_____

The director went home and rested his feet.

_____

Lesson 3 Spatial Organization

When you walk into a room, you naturally look around in an organized way, perhaps from side to side or from near to far. You do not skip from one scattered detail to the next. When writers describe a room or some other place, they should describe it in this same organized way using **spatial organization**. This method helps readers "see" the place just as if they were looking at it themselves. In the description below, Kelli describes her kindergarten classroom from left to right.

I still remember my kindergarten classroom. In the area just to the left of the door, there was a full-sized porch built in the room. This was the meeting area, and we gathered there at the start of each day and during story time. Beyond the porch was the "Building Corner." Stacked there were bins of blocks, cardboard bricks, and plastic tubs. To the right, in the next corner, was the "Learning Corner." We sat at low tables when we had serious work to do, such as writing our first words and sentences. Finally, the last corner, at the far side from the door was the "Creating Corner." Plastic-covered tables were usually lined with wet paintings or crooked clay sculptures. That room seemed like paradise to me.

When organizing ideas spatially, you are using words that tell your reader where things are. Here are some common spatial words.

| above | across | beside | between | beyond | into | left |
| low | middle | next to | over | right | through | under |

Find these or other spatial words in the paragraph above. Write them on the lines below.

_____   _____

_____   _____

_____   _____

_____   _____

Lesson 3 Spatial Organization

Kelli described her kindergarten classroom. What classroom do you remember well? It might be from preschool, or it might be from last year. Describe the room. Choose a method of organization that makes sense. Use sensory details so that readers can see, hear, smell, and feel what is in the room. Remember to use spatial words to tell where things are.

_____

_____

_____

_____

_____

_____

_____

_____

_____

This is Mr. Teachalot. He's been teaching for many years. Your parents haven't met him yet. Describe him for your parents. Organize the details of your description from top to bottom or from bottom to top.

_____

_____

_____

_____

_____

_____

_____

_____

_____

_____

Lesson 4 Describing Objects

When a writer describes an object, readers should be able to see, hear, smell, feel, and perhaps taste it. Think of a familiar food item. Perhaps it's a piece of fruit or an ice cream bar. Consider it as if you are seeing it for the first time. Record its details here. Feel free to consult a thesaurus to find fresh words to describe the item.

Color: _____

Shape: _____

Size:_____

Texture: _____

Smell: _____

Other details:_____

Now, write a paragraph in which you describe the item. Describe it to someone who is not familiar with this food. Remember to appeal to as many of your readers' senses as you can.

_____
_____
_____
_____
_____
_____
_____
_____
_____
_____
_____
_____
_____
_____
_____
_____

Lesson 4 Describing Objects

Now, choose a more complex object. Maybe it's an entire room, or maybe it's an intricate piece of jewelry or a statue. Examine it. Even though it is a familiar object, look at it with fresh eyes. Record details of the object here.

Color: _____

Shape: _____

Size:_____

Texture: _____

Smell: _____

Other details:_____

Now, write a description of the object. Remember to organize your details logically in a side-to-side or top-to-bottom format.

_____

_____

_____

_____

_____

_____

_____

_____

_____

_____

_____

_____

_____

_____

_____

_____

_____

_____

_____

Lesson 5 The Language of Comparison

To compare two things, use the ending **-er** or the word *more* to talk and write about how the two things are different.

The first tulip is *shorter* than the second tulip.

I think the second tulip is *prettier* than the first tulip.

Is the first tulip's stem *slimmer* than the second tulip's stem?

Which tulip do you think is **more** *beautiful*?

- For short words, such as *short*, add **er**.

- For words that end in *y*, change the *y* to *i*, then add **er**.

- For some one-syllable words, such as *slim*, double the final consonant, then add **er**.

- For longer words, such as *beautiful*, use *more* to compare.

Do some more comparing. Look at the pictures and compare them. Use comparative forms of the words in the box in your sentences.

appealing	tall
heavy	yellow

_____

_____

_____

_____

_____

_____

_____

_____

_____

_____

Lesson 5 The Language of Comparison

To talk or write about how three or more things are different, use the ending **-est** or the word *most*.

> The third tulip is the *larg**est*** of the three tulips.

> I still think the second tulip is the *pretti**est*** of the three.

> The first tulip has the *thin**nest*** petals.

> The third tulip is the **most** *fantastic* of these three flowers.

The same spelling changes that occur when you add **er** to a word occur when you add **est** to a word. If you need to, look back at the list on page 34.

Take your turn comparing three objects. Look at the pictures. Use the words in the box to write sentences in which you compare the three objects.

dark	tiny
smooth	unusual

_____

_____

_____

_____

_____

_____

_____

_____

_____

_____

_____

_____

_____

_____

Lesson 6 Comparing Objects

A Venn diagram is a tool that helps writers compare people, ideas, or objects. In the diagram below, moles and rabbits are compared.

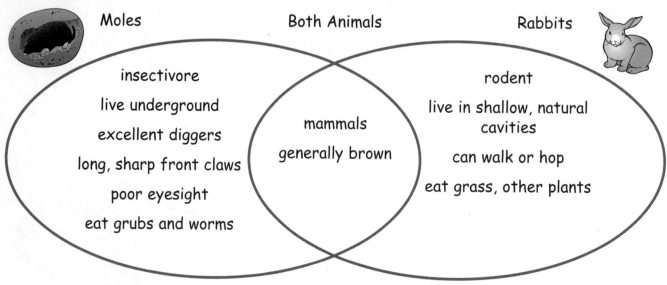

Moles   Both Animals   Rabbits

- insectivore
- live underground
- excellent diggers
- long, sharp front claws
- poor eyesight
- eat grubs and worms

- mammals
- generally brown

- rodent
- live in shallow, natural cavities
- can walk or hop
- eat grass, other plants

To practice using a Venn diagram, compare these two rabbits. Record how each animal is different. Then, write what is the same about the two animals.

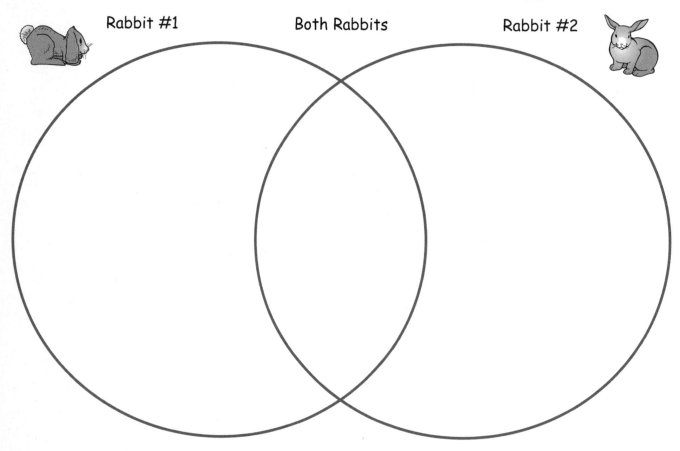

Rabbit #1   Both Rabbits   Rabbit #2

Lesson 6 Comparing Objects

Once you organize ideas in a Venn diagram, you can more easily write about those ideas. When writers write to compare, they must present information in a way that makes sense to readers. There are two ways to organize a written comparison. One way is to talk first about one object, then about the other. This is called a **whole-to-whole comparison**. Here is an example. Information about an orange is in orange. Information about a lemon is in black.

> The orange's thick rind comes off fairly easily. The rind's white insides sometimes coat the outer parts of the orange's sections. Once the orange is peeled, one can easily pull apart the sections. The flavor may be sweet or tart, depending on the orange. The lemon's rind is not usually as thick as that of an orange. It peels as easily, though, and the same white coating may appear on the outer parts of the lemon's sections. The sections pull apart a little less easily. The flavor is sour no matter what type of lemon you have.

The other way to organize a written comparison is to talk first about one feature, or characteristic, as it relates to both objects. Then go on to another feature, and so on. This is a **part-to-part comparison**. Here is an example. Again, information about the orange is in orange; information about the lemon is in black.

> The orange's thick rind comes off fairly easily. The lemon's rind is not usually as thick as that of an orange. It peels as easily, though. The orange rind's white insides sometimes coat the outer parts of the orange's sections. The lemon's white coating may do the same. Once the orange is peeled, one can easily pull apart the sections. The lemon's sections come apart a little less easily. The flavor of an orange may be sweet or tart, depending on the orange. The lemon's flavor, however, is sour no matter what type of lemon you have.

Now, look back at the details you recorded on page 36 about the two rabbits. Write a paragraph in which you compare the two animals. Decide which method of organization you will use: whole-to-whole or part-to-part.

_____
_____
_____
_____
_____
_____
_____
_____

Lesson 7 Comparing Characters

When you read, you probably can't help comparing a book you are reading with others you have read. You may note how situations or characters are alike or different. Comparing characters, whether within a book or among different books, can help you understand a story and its developments.

You already know how to compare things with the help of a Venn diagram. Lu is studying ancient Greek myths. He made this Venn diagram to help identify the different characters.

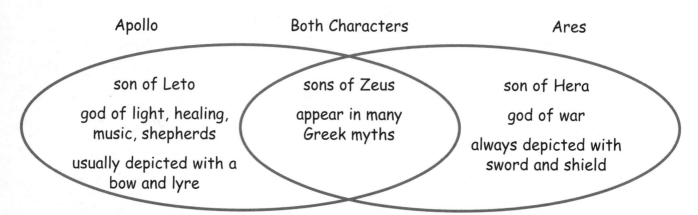

Apollo — Both Characters — Ares

son of Leto

god of light, healing, music, shepherds

usually depicted with a bow and lyre

sons of Zeus

appear in many Greek myths

son of Hera

god of war

always depicted with sword and shield

Think of characters in a book or story you are reading or have read lately. How are they alike and different? Fill out this Venn diagram with what you know about the characters. Think about what the characters think and do, and how they respond to what happens around them. Remember to label the circles with the characters' names.

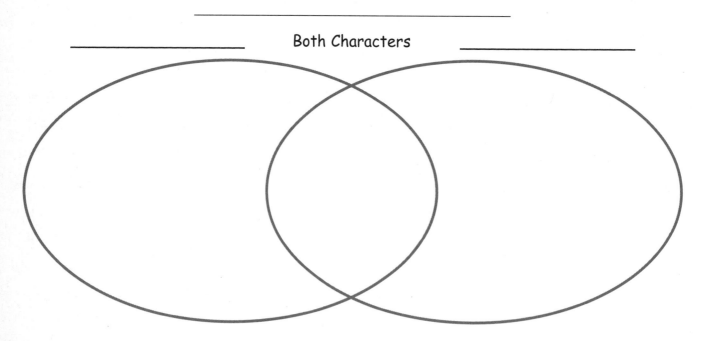

Both Characters

Lesson 7 Comparing Characters

Lu's teacher has asked the students to write about two characters from Greek mythology. Lu reviewed his Venn diagram, then chose part-to-part organization for his paragraph. In other words, he'll talk about one feature of each character, then another feature of each character.

Apollo and Ares are both sons of Zeus, but the similarities stop there. First, they have different mothers. Apollo's mother is Leto; Ares' mother is Hera, the queen of the gods. Apollo has many responsibilities. The myths name him as god of light, healing, music, and shepherds. Ares is the god of war. In art, Apollo is shown with a lyre and a bow, which identify him as protector of flocks. Ares always appears garbed for war, with a sword and shield.

Now, review your own Venn diagram on page 38 and write about your two characters. Decide whether you will use whole-to-whole organization or part-to-part. Look back on pages 36 and 37 to review the two methods, if needed.

_____
_____
_____
_____
_____
_____
_____
_____
_____
_____
_____
_____
_____
_____
_____
_____
_____
_____
_____

Lesson 8 Figurative Language

Descriptive writers use **figurative language** to create vivid images in their readers' minds. Two types of figurative language are similes and metaphors.

In a **simile**, two things that are not alike are compared. A simile always uses the word *like* or *as*.

> After lifting weights all summer, Rick was *as solid as a rock.*

> I, however, was *soft like a marshmallow.*

Complete this sentence to create a simile.

The _____ were as blue as the sky.

Describe something heavy by using the simile "as heavy as lead."

_____

_____

Now, use a simile to compare an autumn tree to the sun.

_____

_____

Compare a flower with a butterfly. Use a simile.

_____

_____

Writers use similes when they want to create a clear or vivid image. They might be found in descriptive writing or in a story.

Choose an object in the room to describe. Tell how it looks, sounds, smells, feels, and/or tastes. Use two similes in your description.

_____

_____

_____

_____

_____

_____

_____

_____

_____

Lesson 8 Figurative Language

A **metaphor** also compares two things that are not alike, but it does not use the words *like* or *as*. In a metaphor, one item is said to be the other item. Here is an example:

The *snow was a blanket*, protecting the tender spring flowers.

If the writer had written, "The snow was *like* a blanket," that would have been a simile. Instead, he used a metaphor and wrote, "The snow was a blanket." The writer could also have simply written, "The snow lay smoothly…". But the blanket metaphor created a more effective image.

Here is another example of a metaphor:

The *lantern moon* hung in the sky.

What two things are being compared in the metaphor above?

_____ and _____

Describe something light (in weight) by comparing the object to a feather. Use a simile.

_____

Use a metaphor to compare a rainbow with a snake.

_____

Writers may use metaphors in many kinds of writing. Janice used one in her personal narrative.

When I was little, the night light in my room was my security blanket. It kept me safe from anything that might have been scary in the night.

Look out a window and describe something that you see. Write how the object looks, smells, sounds, or feels. Use a metaphor or two in your description.

_____

_____

_____

_____

_____

_____

_____

Lesson 9 The Writing Process: Descriptive Writing

Descriptive writing plays a role in many forms of writing. You see it in stories and novels, in textbooks, and in newspaper articles. Use the writing process to develop a paragraph that describes an imaginary place.

Prewrite

Your imaginary place might be your idea of a dream home or a city on a distant planet. The place might be a room, a building, or an outdoor setting. It might be in the past, the present, or the future. Let your imagination go. Write some of your ideas about places here.

_____   _____

_____   _____

_____   _____

Now, look over your list. Which place seems most appealing? Choose one and write the place that you decide on here.

Place I will describe: _____

Use this idea web to record details about your place.

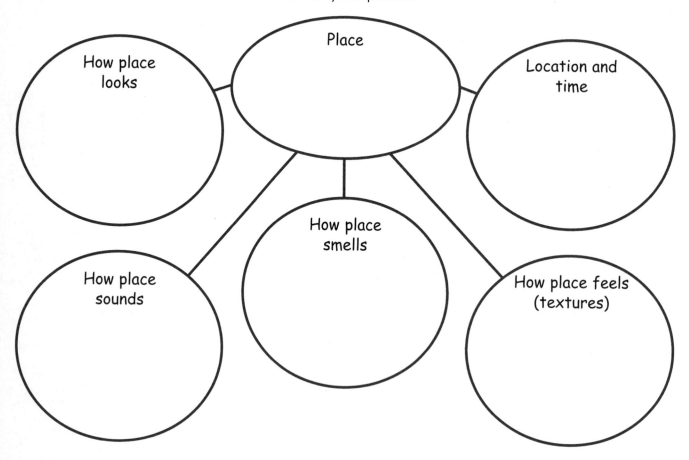

Lesson 9 The Writing Process: Descriptive Writing

As a final step in the prewriting stage, organize your ideas. How will you describe this place? Will you start with a physical description that goes from left to right? Does it make sense to go from bottom to top? Or will you use order of importance to describe the place? Make a choice and record it here.

Method of organization: _____

Major details, in order:

Draft

Refer to your prewriting notes as you write a first draft. Remember, this is the time to get your ideas down on paper in sentences. This is not the time to worry about getting every word exactly right.

_____

_____

_____

_____

_____

_____

_____

_____

_____

_____

Lesson 9 The Writing Process: Descriptive Writing

Revise

Revision is a necessary step in the writing process. Even the most experienced writers know that they may improve their work by carefully reconsidering their message. Reread your draft carefully. Will it be clear to your readers? Will it be interesting? Answer the questions below about your draft. If you answer "no" to any of the questions, then those are the areas that might need improvement.

- Did you keep your audience in mind? Did you include details that will interest them and that they will understand?

- Did you organize your description in a logical way?

- Did you use vivid verbs and precise nouns to help readers see the place?

- Did you use sensory details? To how many of your readers' senses did you appeal?

Rewrite your description here. Make changes to improve your writing, based on the questions you just answered.

_____

_____

_____

_____

_____

_____

_____

_____

_____

_____

_____

_____

_____

_____

_____

_____

_____

Lesson 9 The Writing Process: Descriptive Writing

Proofread

Your description should be in good shape now. The last task is to check it for any remaining errors. It is best to check for one kind of error at a time. Proofread your revision on page 44. Use this checklist to help you catch all of the errors.

_____ Does each sentence begin with a capital letter?

_____ Does each sentence express a complete thought?

_____ Does each sentence have an appropriate end mark?

_____ Are proper nouns (names of people, places, or things) capitalized?

_____ Are all words spelled correctly?

_____ Are commas used correctly?

Publish

Write a final copy of your description here. Use your best handwriting. Be careful not to introduce any new errors.

_____

_____

_____

_____

_____

_____

_____

_____

_____

_____

_____

_____

_____

_____

_____

Chapter 4
Lesson 1 Parts of a Fiction Story

A good story has these ingredients:

- A story tells about made-up people or animals. They are the **characters** in the story.

- A **narrator** tells the story. The narrator might be a character, or the narrator might be a third-person narrator who is not a character.

- A story has a **setting** where the action takes place.

- A story's action is the **plot**. The plot is a series of events that includes a **conflict**, which needs to be resolved.

- A story uses **dialogue**, or conversation among characters, to move the action of the story along.

- **Sensory details** make the characters, setting, and action come alive.

- An interesting **beginning**, **middle**, and **end** make a story fun to read.

Below is the first part of a story. Read it, then answer the questions that follow.

Kler's Quest

The sky glowed green as Kler scuffed to the barn. The dusty ground gave off little puffs with each step. Beside the path, broad flanda leaves shimmered and glowed, almost like the sky. Kler thought about the warm nest she had just left. She thought about what lay ahead of her. It wasn't milking the tambles that she dreaded so much as the skivving of the milk afterward. It took a good two hours to stir it, cook it down, and bottle it. Hopefully, there would be enough for Mother to sell in Tarboon.

Kler hadn't minded the job, at first. Kler's older brother, who used to do the milking, was gone on his quest. He hadn't wanted to go, but Father had made him. The Chief in Tarboon said it was time. Father didn't want to attract attention, so, with what Kler thought was deep regret, Father had sent Fron away.

It had been four months now. Everyone said that was a long time for a quest, but Father didn't seem worried. He bought and sold and tended his tambles, making frequent trips to Tarboon. Father would grow quiet, in between his trips. Then, he would be gone for a few days and return in a more cheerful mood. Kler assumed this had to do with the price of tambles. The uneasy state of affairs in Tarboon didn't enter her mind.

In the warm, earthy barn, the tambles were waiting. They greeted her with high-pitched bleats and playful nips. Kler couldn't help but smile at the feel of their rubbery lips.

Lesson 1 Parts of a Fiction Story

"Good morning, girls," she called out to them. "Yes, I'm here. Make way now." And Kler nudged her way past the long necks of the furry, three-toed beasts to the milking room. The well-mannered animals entered the room four at a time, stood patiently for the milking, and then exited. The milk whirred and swished through pipes as steadily as a ticking clock. Both Kler and the animals knew the routine well.

Today, though, the routine was broken. *CLANK-CLANK.* Kler turned, thinking Mother was returning empty milk bottles. But the barn's dimness revealed no visitors. Kler turned back to scratching her favorite tamble's brow, but another sound caused her to peer into the barn again. A scraping noise came from the darkest corner. The tambles shifted nervously, and a little prickle went up Kler's back. One last tamble skittered aside, and Kler caught her breath.

At the sound, the scraping noise stopped. The huddled figure looked up. The prickle Kler had felt turned into a gut-wrenching blow as she looked at her brother's face. His familiar black eyes stared out of a pale face, but there was nothing in them. Fron had failed his quest. He was blank.

Lesson 1 Parts of a Fiction Story

Answer these questions about "Kler's Quest." Look back at the story on pages 46 and 47 if you need to.

Who is the narrator? _____

Who is the main character in the story?_____

List three details about the main character.

_____ _____ _____

How did you learn these details about the main character?

_____

What other characters appear in the story?

_____

How did you learn about them?_____

Where does the action take place? _____

List some details about the setting.

_____ _____ _____

_____ _____ _____

What kind of problem, or conflict, do you think might occur in this story?

_____

Review the brief dialogue. Notice what the main character says and how she says it. What do you learn about her from the dialogue?

_____

_____

Record some of the story's sensory details. Remember to look for sights, sounds, smells, textures, and tastes.

_____ _____ _____

_____ _____ _____

Lesson 2 Setting

Every story takes place in a certain setting. The setting of a story is when and where the story's action takes place. The setting of a story may be in a real place or in an imaginary place. The time during which a story takes place may be in the past, the present, or the future.

In some stories, the setting is very important. For example, a suspenseful story might rely heavily on the wet, foggy streets of London where the action takes place. In other stories, the characters' thoughts and actions are more important, and the setting is less vital.

Readers learn about a story's setting in different ways. A character might say the name of a town or mention what the weather is like. Or maybe you learn from a character's thoughts that her feet are cold, so you might assume it is winter. In some stories, such as "Kler's Quest," the narrator describes the setting. Here is an example from page 46.

> The sky glowed green as Kler scuffed to the barn. The dusty ground gave off little puffs with each step. Beside the path, broad flanda leaves shimmered and glowed, almost like the sky. Kler thought about the warm nest she had just left. She thought about what lay ahead of her. It wasn't milking the tambles that she dreaded so much as the skivving of the milk afterward. It took a good two hours to stir it, cook it down, and bottle it. Hopefully, there would be enough for Mother to sell in Tarboon.

What details does the narrator reveal about the setting? To which sense does each detail appeal?

Details

_____

_____

_____

_____

_____

_____

Senses

_____

_____

_____

_____

_____

_____

Lesson 2 Setting

Here is another example. This passage is from "The Smallest Dragonboy," by Anne McAffrey. The narrator, who is not a character in the story, reveals details about the setting.

> Keevan glanced upward, past the black mouths of the Weyr caves, in which grown dragons and their chosen riders lived, toward the Star Stones that crowned the ridge of the old volcano that was Benden Weyr. On the height, the blue watch dragon, his rider mounted on his neck, stretched the great transparent pinions that carried him on the winds of Pern to fight the evil Thread that fell at certain times from the skies.

What information do you get about the setting from this passage?

_____

_____

What mood, or feeling, do you feel the details convey?

_____

Writers use details in their settings that match the mood of what is happening in the story. First, think about details that a writer might include in a story that is humorous or light-hearted.

What might the weather be like?

_____

_____

What time of day might it be?

_____

_____

Lesson 2 Setting

Now, think about setting details that a writer might include in a scary part of a story, or in a part where something bad is going to happen to a character.

What might the weather be like?

_____

_____

What time of day might it be?

_____

_____

Look over the details you recorded for "light-hearted" settings and "scary" or "bad" settings. Are you starting to imagine a great story? Choose one of the settings you have already begun to visualize and develop it further here.

Write a paragraph that describes the setting. Indicate both when and where the action takes place. Remember to organize your details in a way that makes sense. For example, if you are describing a distant view, you might go from left to right or from far to near. Think about which method makes most sense for your setting.

_____

_____

_____

_____

_____

_____

_____

_____

_____

_____

_____

_____

_____

Lesson 3 Characters

What makes a good fiction story? One way you might judge is by whether you care about the characters. If the writer makes you care about the characters, then it's probably a story worth reading. Name some characters you remember from stories or novels you have read. Perhaps you remember cheering them on, or at least hoping that things would turn out okay for them.

_____   _____

_____   _____

Now, think about what you know about those characters. How did you learn about them? How did the narrator or author help you get to know the character? Normally, readers learn about characters in four ways:

- The narrator reveals information.

- The character's own words reveal information.

- The character's actions reveal information.

- Other characters' words and actions reveal information.

Review "Kler's Quest," on pages 46 and 47. What do you know about the main character? For each detail you record, write how you know it. For example, in the first sentence you learn that the character has a barn, which suggests a farm-like setting. You know this because the narrator reveals the information.

What I Know About the Character   How I Know It

_____   _____

_____   _____

_____   _____

_____   _____

_____   _____

_____   _____

_____   _____

_____   _____

_____   _____

NAME _____

Lesson 3 Characters

Now, think about a character you would like to create. Rather than thinking about what happens to the character, think about what kind of person the character is. Answer these questions.

Is the character human? _____ If not, what is the character? _____

Is the character male or female?_____

What two words best describe your character?

_____   _____

During what time period does your character live? _____

What background details or family history have "shaped" this character?

_____

What might your character say? How might your character say it? Write a line of dialogue that your character might speak.

_____

What might other characters say about this character? Either write a line of dialogue or describe what others would say.

_____

Now, introduce your character. Write a paragraph about him or her.

_____
_____
_____
_____
_____
_____
_____
_____
_____
_____
_____
_____

Spectrum Writing
Grade 8

Chapter 4 Lesson 3
Writing to Entertain
53

Lesson 4 Dialogue

Dialogue is the conversation among characters in a story. Good dialogue helps readers get to know the characters. Dialogue also moves the action of the story along. Here is what dialogue looks like.

> "Fron?" Kler's voice hardly came out.
>
> The stooping Fron only stared.
>
> Stepping nearer, Kler asked, "Are you okay?" Fron stared.
>
> A shadow at the door startled Kler so that she jumped sideways. There stood Father. He looked, unspeaking, from Kler to Fron and back again.
>
> "Go to the house, Kler," Father said, "and get your mother." His voice was deep and brittle.
>
> "Yes, Father," said Kler, automatically. Then, she couldn't stop her questions. "Father, why is he here? And why does he look like that? What will happen to him?" They all spilled out at once. Father stood silent, still looking back and forth between his two children.
>
> All that he said was, "Speak of this to no one."

What do you learn about Kler, the main character, from this dialogue?

_____

What do you learn about Father?

_____

Take a closer look at a line of dialogue and its punctuation.

Quotation marks go before and after the speaker's exact words.	End punctuation goes inside the quotation marks.

"Go to the house, Kler," Father said, "and get your mother."

A comma separates the speaker's words from the tag line.

Lesson 4 Dialogue

Below is some dialogue that has not been punctuated. Add the punctuation. Look at the dialogue on page 54 for examples if you need to. Consider the use of capital letters as well as the position of quotation marks, commas, and end marks.

Why shouldn't I speak of it Kler asked

Father replied no one must know

What about Kler continued the Chief in Tarboon

Absolutely no one replied Father

Dialogue should sound like real people talking. A 14-year-old character should sound more or less like you sound. A grown-up should sound like a grown-up. Remember, however, that people do sound different from each other. People's speech patterns differ depending on where they grew up, what education they've had, and where they live.

Imagine you meet two 14-year-olds whose parents are the king and queen of a European country. The prince and princess speak excellent English. Imagine a conversation you might have and write the dialogue here. Remember to consider how you would talk to a prince or princess.

_____

_____

_____

_____

_____

_____

_____

_____

_____

_____

_____

_____

_____

_____

Lesson 5 Point of View

When a writer writes a story, he or she chooses a narrator to tell the story. In some stories, the narrator is one of the characters in the story. When this is the case, the story is said to be written in **first-person point of view**. Words such as *I, me,* and *my* let readers know that this is happening. Here is a paragraph from *Jane Eyre,* by Charlotte Brontë. It is written in first-person point of view.

> A small breakfast-room adjoined the drawing-room. I slipped in there. It contained a bookcase: I soon possessed myself of a volume, taking care that it should be one stored with pictures. I mounted into the window-seat: gathering up my feet, I sat cross-legged like a Turk; and, having drawn the red moreen curtain nearly close, I was shrined in double retirement.

Sometimes, an author uses a narrator who is not a character in the story. This type of story, written in **third-person point of view**, may give readers insight into more than one character's thoughts and actions. A narrator who reveals characters' thoughts is omniscient, or all-knowing. Readers see words such as *he, she, him, her, his, they,* and *them* in stories that are written in third person. "Kler's Quest," on pages 46 and 47, has an omniscient third-person narrator. Here is a paragraph from that story.

> Kler hadn't minded the job at first. Kler's older brother, who used to do the milking, was gone on his quest. He hadn't wanted to go, but Father had made him. The Chief in Tarboon said it was time. Father didn't want to attract attention, so, with what Kler thought was deep regret, Father had sent Fron away.

Lesson 5 Point of View

Look back at the paragraph from "Kler's Quest" on page 56. Rewrite the paragraph in first-person point of view, from Kler's point of view.

_____
_____
_____
_____
_____
_____
_____
_____
_____
_____

Now, based on that same paragraph from "Kler's Quest," write a short scene in third-person point of view, from Father's point of view. Let your omniscient narrator reveal what Father might have thought and said about sending Fron on his quest.

_____
_____
_____
_____
_____
_____
_____
_____
_____
_____

Lesson 6 Story Ideas

Many stories are **realistic**. They include human characters who are more or less regular people. Realistic stories set in the past are called **historical fiction**. Whether the setting is in the past or the present, though, the characters could be real, and the events could happen, even though the details come from a writer's imagination.

List some stories or books you have read that have realistic settings.

_____   _____

_____   _____

What kind of realistic story would you like to write? Will it be about a regular kid who accidentally does something amazing? Or might it be about a person who drives a stagecoach? Realistic stories require just as much imagination as unrealistic, or fantasy, stories do. Write down some realistic story ideas.

Realistic story idea #1

Character(s): _____

Setting: _____

Plot: _____

_____

Realistic story idea #2

Character(s): _____

Setting: _____

Plot: _____

_____

Realistic story idea #3

Character(s): _____

Setting: _____

Plot: _____

_____

Lesson 6 Story Ideas

Fiction that is not realistic is called **fantasy**. "Kler's Quest" on pages 46 and 47 is a fantasy. The setting may be anywhere and at any time. Characters may be human or some other life form. Details often involve characters with special powers who go on amazing and dangerous quests, and who are victorious over a "bad" or evil force or enemy.

What fantasy stories have you read? Try to recall some of the details. Were the characters human? Did they have special powers? Did the author specify the setting's place or time period? Record a few details that you remember.

_____   _____

_____   _____

What kind of fantasy would you like to write? Who will be your main characters? What kind of life form are they? Where will they live? Why are they there? What is the time period? Open up your imagination and write down a couple of fantasy ideas here.

Fantasy idea #1

Character(s): _____

Setting: _____

Plot: _____

_____

Fantasy idea #2

Character(s): _____

Setting: _____

Plot: _____

_____

Fantasy idea #2

Character(s): _____

Setting: _____

Plot: _____

_____

NAME _____

Lesson 7 The Writing Process: Fiction Story

Whether a story is realistic or fantasy, it comes from the imagination of the writer. What is in your imagination? Can you imagine a story whose characters are like you and your classmates? Or do your story ideas go far beyond your normal existence? Use the writing process to develop and write a story.

Prewrite

Read the story ideas you sketched out on pages 58 and 59. Choose one of those ideas, or another idea that you like, and begin to develop it. Explore your ideas by filling out this story map. If this idea doesn't work, make another story map on a separate sheet of paper and try again.

Setting
_____
_____

Characters
_____
_____

Plot (Conflict)
_____
_____
_____
_____
_____
_____
_____
_____

Solution
_____
_____

NAME _____

Lesson 7 The Writing Process: Fiction Story

Now that you have developed your story concept, work on your main character. Use this idea web to record details about how he or she looks, acts, speaks, and other details.

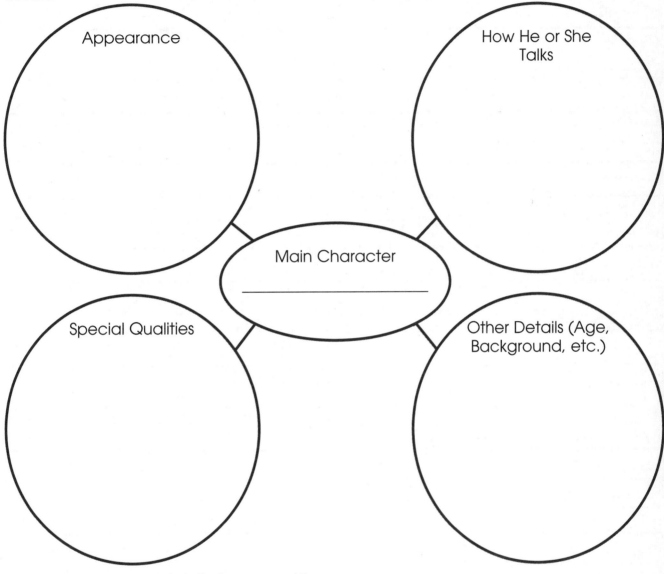

Now, develop some details for your setting.

Location: (planet or country) _____

Location: (type of building, etc.) _____

Time: (year) _____ (season) _____

Appearance: (indoors) _____

Appearance: (outdoors) _____

Lesson 7 The Writing Process: Fiction Story

Now, put the main events of your story together. Think about the story you are about to tell. What is at the beginning, in the middle, and at the end? Refer to the story map you made on page 60. Use the sequence chart on this page to organize the important events in order.

Lesson 7 The Writing Process: Fiction Story

Draft

Write a first draft. Refer to your story map as you work. Continue on another sheet of paper if you need to. As you write, don't worry about mistakes. Just get your ideas down in sentences and in order.

_____

_____

_____

_____

_____

_____

_____

_____

_____

_____

_____

_____

_____

_____

_____

_____

_____

_____

_____

_____

_____

_____

Write some ideas for a title here. You may choose the final title later.

Title:_____

Lesson 7 The Writing Process: Fiction Story

Revise

Revising is a necessary step in the writing process. Even experienced writers find it a challenge. It's hard to change or "fix" something that you worked hard to write.

Answer the questions below. If you answer "no" to any of them, those are the areas you might need to improve. Make marks on your draft so you know what needs attention.

- Did you give details about an interesting character and a setting?
- Does your story have a beginning, a middle, and an end?
- Did you include a problem and a solution in your plot?
- Did you tell events in an order that made sense?
- Did you use sensory details?
- Did you use dialogue to help readers learn about characters and to move the story forward?

Review the important parts of a story.

- In the **beginning** of a story, readers meet the character or characters and learn a little about the setting and the plot. The beginning of a story makes readers want to keep on reading.

- In the **middle** of a story, the action takes place. Readers see the character or characters face a problem. The characters probably make one or more attempts to solve the problem.

- In the **end**, the characters solve the problem in a logical way. Keep in mind that it is not satisfying to have a story's central problem just go away by magic or by coincidence. Your characters must deal with, or solve, their problem.

On your draft, draw brackets next to the beginning, middle, and end of your story. Write some notes if you decide that you must revise any of those parts to make them more interesting for your readers.

Lesson 7 The Writing Process: Fiction Story

Read your draft out loud. Listen for awkward sentences or sentences that sound alike. Then, write the revision of your story here. Fix any awkward sentences as you go.

_____

_____

_____

_____

_____

_____

_____

_____

_____

_____

_____

_____

_____

_____

_____

_____

_____

_____

_____

_____

_____

_____

_____

_____

_____

Review your title choices. Which one seems best? Write it here.

Title: _____

Lesson 7 The Writing Process: Fiction Story

Proofread

By now, you have read your story several times through and are very familiar with it. It is still important, though, to proofread carefully. When you are familiar with what you are reading, you are more likely to overlook errors. Also, you must still proofread typewritten text, even if the computer has checked your spelling. If you type *form* instead of *from*, for example, only you can catch that error. Use the checklist below as you proofread your revised story. Read for one kind of error at a time.

> _____ Each sentence begins with a capital letter.
>
> _____ Each sentence ends with the correct punctuation.
>
> _____ Each sentence states a complete thought.
>
> _____ All words are spelled correctly.

Use the proofreaders' symbols to mark your corrections and revisions. Remember to read your writing out loud. When you read out loud, you may hear mistakes or rough spots that you did not see.

> • Capitalize this letter.
>
> • Add a missing end mark: ⊙ ? !
>
> • Add a comma please.
>
> • "Be sure to punctuate your dialogue," she said.
>
> • Fix incorrect or misspelled words.
>
> • Delete this word.
>
> • Lowercase this letter.

Lesson 7 The Writing Process: Fiction Story

Publish

Write a final copy of your story on the next page. Continue on another sheet of paper if you need to. Write carefully so that there are no mistakes. Share your story with friends and family.

_____

_____

_____

_____

_____

_____

_____

_____

_____

_____

_____

_____

_____

_____

_____

_____

_____

_____

_____

_____

_____

_____

Chapter 5

Lesson 1 Persuasive Writing

A persuasive writer tries to make readers think, feel, or act in a certain way. An advertisement tries to make you think you "need" a product. A fundraiser might persuade you to feel sorry for flood victims so that you will donate money. A campaign brochure might persuade you to vote for a candidate.

In the persuasive article below, the writer shares her opinions, then gives some information. Finally, she asks her readers to take action.

Around Town

Jade Greening, Guest Columnist

The city planners are telling us we need to expand East Morgan Avenue from four to six lanes. They say the traffic is too congested. They say it will be better for business. I drove over to see for myself.

In case you haven't been there for a while, that stretch of East Morgan Avenue has lots of little shops and eateries. People like to wander from shop to shop, then stop and eat, then wander some more. That's what I did, and it was thoroughly pleasant.

I spent an entire afternoon and evening in the area. The traffic did not seem congested. I couldn't figure out what all the excitement was about. So, I did a little digging.

Two members on the city planning board are business owners. The companies they own are developing a large retail mall east of town at the far end of Morgan Avenue. Is it possible that they want East Morgan Avenue expanded to benefit their own interests? Let's not ruin the East Morgan Avenue neighborhood for the sake of this other new retail mall. Talk to your city representatives. Make it clear that you want East Morgan Avenue to stay as it is.

What action does the writer ask readers to take?

_____

_____

_____

_____

Lesson 1 Persuasive Writing

Changes occur in every town and city. What change is your community facing? Perhaps there is a debate about closing a landfill or building a new school. Maybe new housing developments are springing up all over what used to be farmers' fields, or maybe graffiti or roadside trash is a problem. Identify a local issue that interests you. Write a persuasive article as if you are a guest columnist for your local newspaper. Identify the issue, state your opinions, and call for your readers to take a specific action.

_____

_____

_____

_____

_____

_____

_____

_____

_____

_____

_____

_____

_____

_____

_____

_____

_____

_____

_____

_____

_____

_____

_____

_____

Lesson 2 Facts and Opinions

Which of these sentences is a fact? Which is an opinion?

> Our city does a good job of maintaining the streets.

> City road crews spent 187 hours filling potholes this spring.

If you're not sure, ask yourself these questions: Which statement could be proven true? That would be a **fact**. Which is a belief or a personal judgment? That would be an **opinion**.

Often, writers state both facts and opinions. That is okay, but both writers and readers must be able to tell the difference between the two. Look for facts and opinions as you read this article about the expansion of East Morgan Avenue.

From the Editor's Desk

City records indicate that daily traffic on East Morgan Avenue has increased by 24 percent in the last five years. Considering the increase in population in that part of town, the increase in traffic is not a surprise. City planners tell us the road needs to be expanded to six lanes. They say it is congested. They say that the taxpayers of this city should support this multi-million-dollar project.

I believe that the taxpayers should support this expansion. As the main east-west artery through our city, the road is highly traveled by residents and visitors alike. It is in the city's best interest to improve and dress up East Morgan Avenue. Our civic pride should kick in. When it comes time to vote on this issue, we must vote "yes" for the sake of our city.

Words such as *think, believe, should, must, never, always, seems, like, hate, best,* and *worst* may signal that a statement is an opinion. Read the article again and circle any opinion signal words you find.

Lesson 2 Facts and Opinions

Write two facts from the article on page 70.

_____

_____

Write two opinions from the article.

_____

_____

Mr. Lewis has his own opinion about the East Morgan Avenue issue. He wrote an e-mail to his brother, who lives across town. Read this paragraph from his e-mail.

> I think this move to expand East Morgan Avenue is nuts. Expanding to six lanes puts the road right up against the storefronts. Those historic buildings will never handle that kind of stress. This is the worst idea the city planners have come up with yet. I believe that expanding Morgan Avenue would absolutely ruin that neighborhood. Be sure to tell your neighbors to voice their disapproval of this plan.

Write one fact from Mr. Lewis's paragraph.

_____

Circle any opinion signal words that you find in Mr. Lewis's text. Then, write one opinion that he states.

_____

Now, form your own opinion about East Morgan Avenue. If this were happening in your town or neighborhood, what side of the issue would you be on? State your opinion here.

_____

_____

_____

_____

Lesson 3 Emotional Appeals

How do persuasive writers get readers to think, feel, or act in a certain way? Often, they appeal to readers' emotions. When writers make an **emotional appeal**, they mention things about which readers feel strongly. For example, Tina Marple owns a business on East Morgan Avenue. She wrote a letter to the editor about the proposed expansion of the street.

> I have been in business on East Morgan Avenue for 12 years. Everything I have is invested in my diner. My customers count on the relaxed, quiet atmosphere of my diner and of the neighborhood. Widening Morgan Avenue would completely ruin me. This proposal would deprive me of my livelihood.

Ms. Marple knows that most people feel strongly about other people who just want to make a decent, honest living. Though she states many opinions, rather than facts, the opinions have a strong emotional appeal and may persuade readers to believe as she does.

Many people have strong feelings about issues such as these:

justice	family	safety	education
money	home	security	violence
injustice	crime	waste	
tradition	progress	conservation	

What makes you mad when you listen to the news or read a newspaper? What makes you feel good? Name some issues about which you have strong feelings.

_____   _____
_____   _____
_____   _____
_____   _____
_____   _____
_____   _____
_____   _____

Lesson 3 Emotional Appeals

Read the letter to the editor below. What kind of emotional appeal does the writer make?

Dear Editor:

In response to the letter from Tina Marple (printed on 4/12), I must say that she is not looking at the big picture. If her diner is any good, her clients will continue to go there. People don't go to a diner because of the neighborhood; people go to a diner for the food.

Anyone can see that widening Morgan Avenue will benefit everyone. The expansion will make for easier access to all the businesses on the east end of town. People who refuse to make way for progress might as well go back to thinking the world is flat.

J. Alvarez

Explain the emotional appeal in Mr. Alvarez's letter to the editor.

_____

_____

_____

_____

Write a letter to the editor in response to Mr. Alvarez's letter. Write in support of his opinion, or indicate why you disagree with him, and tell why. Remember to consider your audience. What kind of emotional appeal might make people agree with you?

Dear Editor:

_____

_____

_____

_____

_____

_____

_____

_____

_____

_____

_____

_____

_____

_____

_____

_____

Lesson 3 Advertising

Advertising is all about emotional appeals. Advertisers count on strong feelings that people have about wanting to feel good, to fit in, to feel secure, and to have fun. They use a combination of words and images to persuade readers.

Here is the logo for Tina's Hometown Diner. Why do you think she chose that slogan and image?

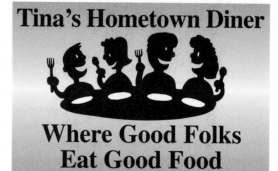

_____

_____

_____

_____

For advertising copywriters, **audience** is especially important. Perhaps the most often-asked questions are these: Who might buy this product? What kind of message can persuade them to buy?

You are an advertising copywriter. Think up a slogan for a fitness club. First, think about who the audience is. About what kinds of issues might they have strong feelings? Give the club a name. Create a slogan that makes an emotional appeal. Sketch the image you would include with the slogan. Your slogan and image should work together to make a strong emotional appeal. Create your ad in this space.

Lesson 4 Order of Importance

When you write about events, you use time order. When you describe a place, you use spatial order. When you write to persuade, you should use **order of importance**.

Remember, persuasive writers try to make their readers think or act in a certain way. As you persuade, save your most important ideas—your strongest arguments—for last. So, build ideas from least important to most important.

Here is part of an e-mail that a concerned citizen wrote to the school board. Notice the reasons she gives for not adjusting the school day.

Everyone is talking about the money the school district will save by adjusting the school-day schedules. By having the middle and high schools begin at 7:30 a.m., buses can pick up and deliver those children, then re-do the routes for the elementary children, whose school day would begin at 8:30. This schedule would allow the district to use fewer buses. On the surface, saving money is a good thing. What about the other ramifications of this plan?

If school started at 7:30, some bus routes would begin as early as 6 a.m. Research shows that teenagers' bodies need more sleep. Getting up at 5 a.m. will not benefit 13- to 19-year-olds. The new schedule would release these same children at 2:30 p.m. That means a whole extra hour for many children to be on their own before parents get home from work. Finally, there is a safety issue. In many families, parents depart for work and leave older children responsible for younger children. If older children get on the bus an hour earlier, some younger children may be left unsupervised. Leaving young children unsupervised is not safe, but finding an alternative creates hardships for these families.

The school board should look for ways to save money, but I call on the board to make wise decisions about the health and safety of our children.

The writer gave several reasons for why the school-day schedule should not be changed. Number the reasons in the paragraph. Then, underline the most important reason.

Lesson 4 Order of Importance

When does your school day start? What if the school board wanted to make it an entire hour earlier? They say it would save money and that it would create more opportunities for after-school activities. Would you be for or against such a plan? Write to the school board. Tell them what you think and why. Ask yourself what will persuade the board to agree with you.

Before you begin drafting your letter, write your reasons here. Then, number them in the order in which you will use them in your letter. Save the strongest argument, or the most important reason, for last.

Reason: _____

Reason: _____

Reason: _____

Reason: _____

Dear _____,

Lesson 5 Letters of Request and Complaint

A **business letter** is a letter written to a company, organization, or person you do not know. People write business letters for many reasons. Two common reasons are to request something and to make a complaint.

In a **letter of request**, the writer asks for something, usually information. The tone is polite, and the writer expresses gratitude for the recipient's time and help.

In a **letter of complaint**, the writer expresses a complaint, then asks the recipient to do something. It is important to be very clear about the action the recipient should take. The tone of complaint letters should be calm and matter-of-fact. As with all persuasive writing, the writer's goal is to get the recipient to agree with his or her own views.

Both types of letter follow the same format. Read the letter of request below. Note the letter's six parts.

The **heading** includes the sender's address and the date.	27557 Fireweed Drive Fresno, CA 93778 October 10, 2008
The **inside address** is the name and address of the recipient.	Caltrans Adopt-A-Highway Department P.O. Box 12616 Fresno, CA 93778
A colon follows the **greeting**.	Dear Sir or Madam:
The text of the letter is the **body**.	I am a member of Girl Scout Troop # 424. We are dedicated to helping our community and to making the world a better place to be. Our troop would like to learn about adopting a section of highway to help keep it clean. Please send information about the Adopt-A-Highway program and a permit application.
The first word of the **closing** is capitalized, and a comma follows the last word.	Thank you,
The sender always includes a **signature**.	*Melanie Feinstein* Melanie Feinstein

Lesson 5 Letters of Request and Complaint

What kind of information would you like to request? Perhaps you would like to learn about a historical figure from a local museum or historical society. Or maybe you have a question about a specific animal at the zoo. Write a letter of request. Make your request clear and remember to include the six parts of a business letter.

Lesson 5 Letters of Request and Complaint

Imagine you just bought a new coat, and the zipper doesn't work. The coat was from a clearance rack, and the store won't take it back. So, you write a letter of complaint to the company that made the coat. Be sure to make a reasonable, clear request at the end so the recipient knows what action you expect. Follow the business letter format.

NAME _____

Lesson 6 The Writing Process: Persuasive Article

Our schools, neighborhoods, and communities change, whether we want them to or not. What is happening in your community that is good and bad? Use the writing process to plan and write a persuasive article about a local issue about which you have strong feelings.

Prewrite

Think about issues about which you feel strongly. What would you like to have happen, or what change would you like to bring about? Make notes here.

_____   _____

_____   _____

_____   _____

Now, think about these issues for a few minutes. About which one do you feel most strongly? Choose the issue you will write about.

_____

Use this idea web to collect your feelings about this issue. Think about why you are unsatisfied or why you want change. You may state opinions, but you must also give reasons or facts. Also, consider what action you expect readers to take. Add more ovals to the idea web if you need to.

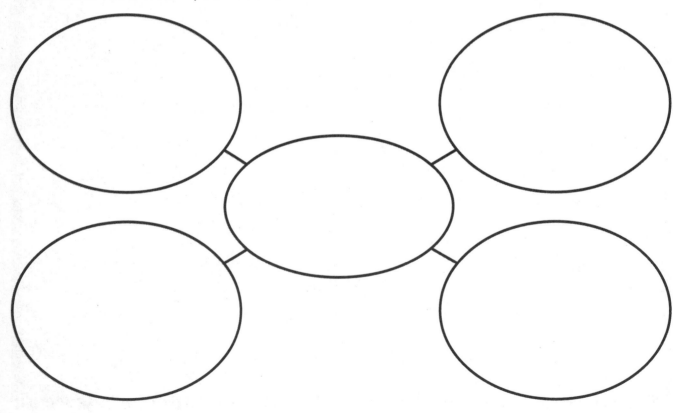

Lesson 6 The Writing Process: Persuasive Article

Now, it is time to organize the points you will make in your persuasive article. What is your strongest argument? Save that one for last. Write your important reasons or points in order in these boxes.

Lesson 6 The Writing Process: Persuasive Article

Draft

Write a first draft of your article on this page. Refer to your chart on page 81. As you write, don't worry about spelling or punctuation. Just get your ideas down in sentences and in order.

_____

_____

_____

_____

_____

_____

_____

_____

_____

_____

_____

_____

_____

_____

_____

_____

_____

_____

_____

_____

_____

_____

_____

Lesson 6 The Writing Process: Persuasive Article

Revise

Even experienced writers change and improve upon their drafts. Reread your own work slowly and carefully. Then, answer the questions below about your draft. If you answer "no" to any of these questions, those are the areas that might need improvement. Feel free to make marks on your draft so you know what needs more work.

> • Did you state your opinion clearly?
>
> • Did you give strong reasons to support your opinion?
>
> • Did you organize those reasons in a logical order, such as least important to most important?
>
> • Did you clearly state what you want readers to think or do?

With persuasive writing, it is especially important to aim your arguments at your specific audience. Ask yourself these questions.

- What opinions do my audience already hold about this issue?
- What does my audience already know about this issue?
- What will they need to know in order to understand the issue?
- What emotional appeals might sway the audience in my direction?

Read your work out loud during the revision stage. Hearing the words might help you to catch awkward sentences or ideas that don't flow smoothly.

Lesson 6 The Writing Process: Persuasive Article

Write your revised article here. As you revise, remember to keep your audience in mind.

_____

_____

_____

_____

_____

_____

_____

_____

_____

_____

_____

_____

_____

_____

_____

_____

_____

_____

_____

_____

_____

_____

_____

_____

_____

_____

_____

_____

_____

_____

Lesson 6 The Writing Process: Persuasive Article

Proofread

Now it is time to correct any last little mistakes. You will be a better proofreader if you read for just one kind of error at a time. So, read for capital letters first, then look for end punctuation, then for spelling, and so on. Here is a checklist to use as you proofread your revised article.

> ____ Each sentence begins with a capital letter.
>
> ____ Each sentence is punctuated correctly.
>
> ____ Each sentence states a complete thought.
>
> ____ All words are spelled correctly.

When proofreaders work, they use certain symbols. These symbols will make your job easier.

Use these symbols as you proofread your article. Remember to read your writing out loud, just as you did at the revising stage. You may hear mistakes or rough spots that you did not catch just by reading your work.

- Capitalize this letter.
- Write in a missing end mark like this: ⊙ ? !
- Insert a comma please.
- Fix incorret or misspelled words like this.
- Delete this word.
- Lowercase this letter.

Publish

Write or type a final copy of your article on a separate sheet of paper. Work carefully and neatly so that there are no mistakes. Remember that if you use a computer, you still need to proofread your work. A spell-check program can catch some errors, but it may miss others.

Chapter 6
Lesson 1 Explanatory Writing

Some explanatory writing is simple. A sign says "Exit," and you know how to get out of a building. Some explanations are not simple. A digital camera, for example, comes with a whole book full of instructions. That new computer desk your dad just bought came in 47 pieces, with instructions to assemble the parts using only one handy tool.

Some explanatory writing does not take the form of instructions, though. Some explanations tell how or why something happened. For example, your teacher might explain events that lead up to World War I. You might read an explanation of what caused the Great Depression. Or your coach might explain a new warm-up drill.

List some explanations that you have read or heard this week. Think about your science, health, and history classes.

_____   _____

_____   _____

_____   _____

Think about instructions you have read or used. How many different kinds can you list?

_____   _____

_____   _____

_____   _____

When you write to explain, or give instructions, you might write for these reasons:

- to tell how to make something
- to tell how something works
- to tell how to get somewhere
- to tell why something happened

Lesson 1 Explanatory Writing

Here is a simple explanation that tells how to clean a sink.

First, remove any items from the sink and countertop. Rinse the sink, and dampen a sponge. Then, sprinkle or squirt cleanser around the sink bowl. Scrub all surfaces of the sink, countertop, and faucet with the sponge. Next, rinse the sponge and all surfaces with hot water. Finally, dry the sink and countertop and polish the faucet with a clean, dry rag or towel.

The writer stated each step in order. To help readers follow the steps, she used order words such as *first, then, next,* and *finally* to make the order clear. Underline each of those order words that you find in the paragraph, above.

What do you know how to do? Write down a few simple processes, such as cleaning a sink, that you think you can explain clearly.

_____   _____

_____   _____

Now, choose one of the processes you listed and think carefully about each of its steps. Imagine that you are explaining the process to someone who has never done it before. You will have to start at the very beginning. List the steps here.

Process: _____

Step 1: _____

Step 2: _____

Step 3: _____

Step 4: _____

Step 5: _____

Step 6: _____

Step 7: _____

Step 8: _____

Step 9: _____

Step 10: _____

Step 11: _____

Step 12: _____

Step 13: _____

Lesson 2 Cause-and-Effect Relationships

Why do dogs chew on things? Why do some kids like math and others don't? When you ask why, you are looking for causes. A **cause** is a reason that something happens. An **effect** is a thing that happens. Here are some examples of causes and effects. Think about the relationship between each cause and effect.

Cause	Effect
I stepped in a puddle.	My shoes are wet.
My pocket has a hole.	My loose change fell out.
I stuffed my shirt into a drawer.	The shirt is wrinkled.

When writers write to explain, they often use causes and effects. They use words and phrases such as *so, because, as a result,* and *therefore* to link causes and effects. Read the paragraph below about life during the 1930s. Circle the cause-and-effect words and phrases in the paragraph.

Drought and poor farming practices caused the Dust Bowl. Prior to the 1930s, the Plains grasslands of Colorado, Kansas, Oklahoma, Texas, and New Mexico had been plowed and planted with wheat. During years of plenty rainfall, the land produced well. During drought, however, it did not. Still, the farmers kept plowing, planting, and hoping. After several years of drought, several crops had failed, so there was nothing left to hold the soil in place. As a result, when winds swept across the Plains, they simply blew the topsoil away, creating what is known as the *Dust Bowl*. The skies were sometimes darkened for days at a time because of the dust clouds.

Can you find some causes and effects in that paragraph? One is written for you. Write two other causes and effects.

Cause	Effect
drought, poor farming practices	Dust Bowl

Lesson 2 Cause-and-Effect Relationships

Writers might also use causes and effects when they tell about events that happened in a story or novel. Here are some causes and effects from *The True Confessions of Charlotte Doyle* by Avi.

It is summer break, so 13-year-old Charlotte Doyle is free from her English boarding school. Her father has arranged for her to sail to America. Everyone feels it is safe for young Charlotte because her father's company owns the ship and because the ship's captain has a good reputation. However, Charlotte's traveling companions—trusted friends of the family—do not show up. As a result, Charlotte is the only passenger on the long voyage across the Atlantic.

Find the causes and effects in the paragraph above. Write them here. The first one is done for you.

Cause	Effect
It is summer break.	Charlotte is free from school.

Think about a story or novel you have read recently. What happened, and what did the characters do? Think about the events in terms of causes and effects. Ask yourself questions such as these: What caused this event to happen? What effect did this event have?

Write the causes and effects of some important events from the book.

Book title: _____

Cause	Effect

Lesson 2 Cause-and-Effect Relationships

In science class, you read about things, you conduct experiments, you observe, and you write about what you learn. Many of the things that you learn in science are causes and effects. For example, you learn what causes rain. Or you learn what happens when a pond becomes polluted.

When you write about what you learn in science, the causes and effects should be clear. Below are two simple experiments. You have probably done them or seen them done. Read about them, then choose one to write about.

Experiment 1

Plant bean seeds in two foam cups. Keep the soil in Cup 1 moist by watering a little bit each day. In Cup 2, water thoroughly only once a week. Record when each seed sprouts. Measure the rate of growth of the seedlings.

Experiment 2

Put 5 drops of blue food coloring in a cup with 8 ounces of water. Place a stalk of celery in the cup. Observe. Record the rate at which the celery "drinks" the water.

Now, imagine that you have done one of the experiments. You made observations and took notes. Now, write a summary of the experiment. What happened? Why did it happen? What happened next?

Experiment # _____

_____

_____

_____

_____

_____

_____

_____

_____

_____

_____

Lesson 2 Cause-and-Effect Relationships

The study of history is also about causes and effects. One event happens, and it is the cause of several other events. And each of those events causes any number of other events.

Reread the paragraph about the Dust Bowl on page 88. Many droughts have occurred in the past, and many places in the world are experiencing drought today. The one that hit the southern Plains in 1931 had vast consequences. Answer these questions based on what you know or think.

What causes a drought? _____

_____

How would a drought affect farmers? _____

_____

What might farmers have to do during a long drought?

_____

_____

Could a drought affect a whole country? If not, why not? If so, how?

_____

_____

_____

Now, write a paragraph in which you describe the causes and effects of drought on an area. Be sure to use words and phrases such as *so*, *because*, *as a result*, and *therefore* to link causes and effects.

_____

_____

_____

_____

_____

_____

_____

_____

_____

_____

Lesson 3 Report an Event

In a news report, you hear about an event. Maybe there was a community meeting, a softball play-off, or a traffic accident. In addition to relating events in the order in which they occurred, the reporter links causes and effects. Causes and effects help readers understand what happens and why.

Here is part of a report about an event. Look for words that signal cause-and-effect relationships: *so, because, as a result, therefore.* When you find them, circle them.

The spring primary election is only a month away, so the Election Board hosted a "Meet the Candidates" night. Several hundred people attended the event held in the courthouse annex. The race for state representative is hotly contested, so many people were eager to hear what the two candidates—Vern Tincher and Carla Kimura—had to say. Because of a sudden illness, however, Tincher was unable to attend. As a result, Kimura hinted to the crowd that Tincher was getting too old to do his job well. This comment resulted in nods of consent from a number of citizens.

Write three causes and three effects from the paragraph.

Cause: _____   Effect: _____

_____   _____

Cause: _____   Effect: _____

_____   _____

Cause: _____   Effect: _____

_____   _____

Lesson 3 Report an Event

Now, think about causes and effects in an event in your own life. What happened during first period? What happened on the way to lunch? Even if nothing exciting happened, there were causes and effects in action. What did you do? What happened next? What resulted from these happenings? List some events in order. Draw arrows to show any cause-and-effect relationship among events.

1. _____
2. _____
3. _____
4. _____
5. _____

Now, practice writing about causes and effects. Write a paragraph about the happenings you listed above. Remember to use *so, because, as a result*, and *therefore* to connect the cause-and-effect relationships.

_____
_____
_____
_____
_____
_____
_____
_____
_____
_____
_____
_____
_____
_____
_____
_____
_____

Lesson 4 Graphics and Visual Aids

The school fundraiser is over. The money is all collected. Now, it is time to print the results of the sale. Which class sold the most light bulbs? Someone prepares an article with the results for the school newspaper.

> The results of the school fundraiser appear below. The results are reported alphabetically, by homeroom teacher's name, and by grade, starting with sixth grade.
> For sixth grade, Mrs. Barbieri's class sold 321 light bulbs. Mr. Domlin's class sold 185 light bulbs. Mr. Krautkramer's class sold 289. Ms. Nuñez's class sold 248. Mrs. Pawley's class sold 203 light bulbs. Ms. Quillen's class sold 236, and Ms. Thatcher's class sold 278 light bulbs.

You can see where this is going. Lots of words and numbers. What if the writer had presented the information in a visual way? Here's the sixth-grade fundraiser information shown in a bar graph.

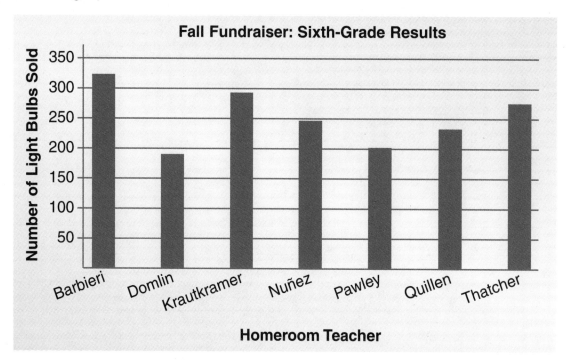

Whose class sold the most light bulbs? You can see at a glance, can't you. Graphics show you in a moment what might take minutes to find in a complicated paragraph of text. Graphics may take the form of drawings, photographs, maps, graphs, or diagrams. The form depends on what type of information the writer is trying to convey.

Lesson 4 Graphics and Visual Aids

A bar graph is just one way to show information in a visual way. Diagrams, line graphs, circle graphs, and pictographs are also good tools. Here is a line graph that shows how much money the school has raised in each of its last five fundraisers.

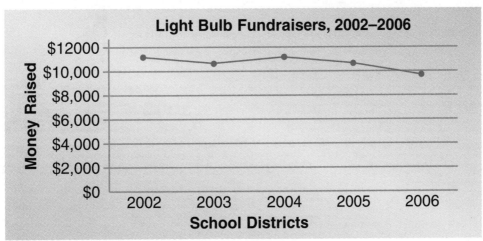

Now, create your own visual aid. Suppose you are keeping track of how many people in your class wear blue denim jeans each day. Or perhaps your own school is having a fundraiser or a charity drive. Record the number of items your class collects or sells. Think about how you could show the information in a creative and meaningful way with a table or graph. Acquire or make up data, if necessary, and write it in this space.

Data

Now, create your graphic here.

Lesson 5 Directions

It seems that it's always a bad sign when you get directions from someone, and the person finishes up by saying, "You can't miss it." So, you go out the door, down the hall, around the corner, and...you've missed it.

If you were in a familiar place and someone asked you for directions, would you be able to give clear directions? Directions need to be in order. As you write them, think about what must happen first, second, next, and so on. In addition, directions need to tell "where." Here are some words that are often used in directions.

Time-Order Words	Direction Words	Position Words
first	up	over
second	down	under
then	left	past
next	right	beyond
after that	south	before
finally	northeast	above
		beside

Here is how Misha told his friend's mom to get to the hobby store that sells the models the boys collect. Underline the time-order, direction, and position words in the paragraph.

First, you have to take the Red Line train downtown. Get off at the 67th Street station. Then, go to the exit at the east end of the station. At the exit, turn left. Walk two blocks to Trader Avenue. Turn right and go over the bridge. Just past the bridge on the right side is a store with a bright green front. That is Mike's Hobby Shop.

Lesson 5 Directions

Write directions that tell how to get from one place to another in your neighborhood. If you need to, close your eyes and imagine yourself walking from one place to the other. Now, write your directions. Look back to page 96 to review time-order, direction, and position words.

_____

_____

_____

_____

_____

_____

_____

_____

Imagine you and a friend once buried treasure on an island. Write directions so that if the map gets lost, you can find the way to the treasure. If you wish, make a sketch of the island on a separate sheet of paper.

_____

_____

_____

_____

_____

_____

_____

_____

_____

_____

_____

Lesson 6 The Writing Process: How-to Instructions

Use the writing process to see how good you are at explaining to someone else how to do something.

Prewrite

Think about things that you know how to do. You might think about using a digital camera, about playing a card or board game, or about making your favorite food. Write down some things that you know how to do or make.

_____   _____

_____   _____

_____   _____

Look over your list and imagine explaining how to do each thing. With which topic are you most comfortable? Explore the idea by writing down everything you can think of about that topic. Add your details to this idea web.

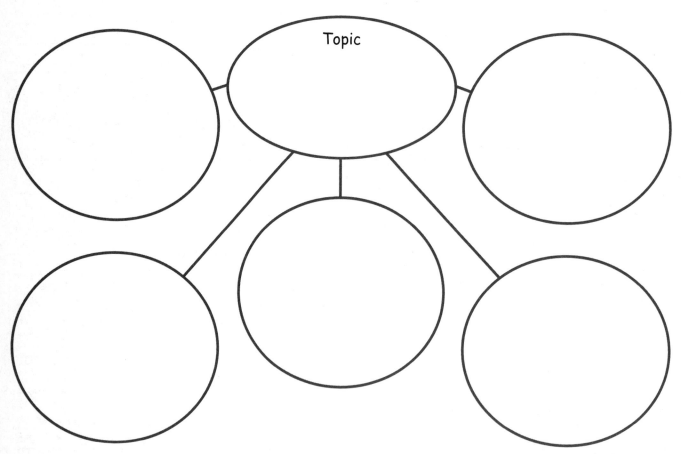

Topic

Are you comfortable with your topic? If not, go back to your list and choose another. Explore it with an idea web on a separate sheet of paper. Remember to think about your audience. What will they need to know?

Lesson 6 The Writing Process: How-to Instructions

Now, it is time to put the steps of your instructions in order. Think about the process you are about to explain. Your audience has never done this before, so you need to start at the very beginning. Use the sequence chart on this page to list the important steps in your explanation. Don't worry about details here; just be sure to list the main steps in the correct order.

1. _____

2. _____

3. _____

4. _____

5. _____

6. _____

7. _____

8. _____

9. _____

Lesson 6 The Writing Process: How-to Instructions

Draft

On this page, write a first draft of your instructions. Keep your sequence chart on hand as you write. Continue on another sheet of paper if you need to. As you write, don't worry about whether everything is perfect. You will have a chance to revise and improve later.

_____

_____

_____

_____

_____

_____

_____

_____

_____

_____

_____

_____

_____

_____

_____

_____

_____

_____

_____

_____

_____

Lesson 6 The Writing Process: How-to Instructions

Revise

Though you are very familiar with your own work, try to reread it with fresh eyes. Even experienced writers do this, and most agree that revising is harder work than writing the first draft. Answer the questions below about your draft. If you answer "no" to any questions, those are the areas that might need improvement. Make marks on your draft, so you know what needs more work.

- Did you explain how to do something from beginning to end?

- Did you include all of the steps in order?

- Did you include time-order words to make the sequence clear?

- Did you use direction and position words to make your details clear?

- Did you use good describing words so your readers can "see" what they are supposed to do?

- Did you keep your audience in mind by asking yourself what they might already know or what they need to know?

- Did you include a heading or title so readers know what they are reading about?

Recognizing causes and effects helps readers understand what they are reading. The words *so, because, therefore,* and *as a result* may signal cause-and-effect relationships. Here is an example:

I like to make birthday cards because I can make each one unique. My friend, Rachel, likes cats, so her card was all about cats. Trudy is into books, so her card was a mini-book. Because Marshall is a big basketball fan, the saying on his card sounded like a game commentator.

Look back at your draft and think about cause-and-effect relationships. Are the causes and effects clear? Do you need to add signal words to make them more clear?

Lesson 6 The Writing Process: How-to Instructions

Write the revision of your instructions here. As you revise, remember to think about important details that your readers will need to know.

_____

_____

_____

_____

_____

_____

_____

_____

_____

_____

_____

_____

_____

_____

_____

_____

_____

_____

_____

_____

_____

_____

_____

_____

_____

Lesson 6 The Writing Process: How-to Instructions

Proofread

Now it is time to correct any last little mistakes. Good proofreaders look for just one kind of error at a time. So, read through once for capital letters. Read again for end punctuation. Read again for spelling, and so on. Here is a checklist to use as you proofread your instructions.

_____ Each sentence begins with a capital letter.

_____ Each sentence is punctuated correctly.

_____ Each sentence states a complete thought.

_____ All words are spelled correctly.

Use standard proofreading symbols as you proofread your own revised instructions.

As you proofread, remember to read your writing out loud, even if there is no one to listen. When you read, you may hear mistakes or awkward spots that you did not see.

- Capitalize this letter.

- Add a missing end mark: ⊙ ? !

- Insert a comma‸please.

- Fix incorrect or misspelled words.

- Delete this word.

- Lowercase this Letter.

Publish

Write a final copy of your instructions on a separate sheet of paper. Write or type carefully and neatly so that there are no mistakes. If you wish, include a graph, chart, or diagram to enhance your instructions and to make them more clear. Read your instructions out loud, or perform a demonstration for an audience.

Chapter 7

NAME _____

When you write a report for a teacher, you present information about a topic. You do this to show what you know or to show what you have learned. Here is a report that Cayden wrote for his American history class.

Rosie the Riveter

In 1943, the War Manpower Commission and the Office of War Information began a campaign. Campaign posters showed a character called "Rosie the Riveter," an attractive, yet almost brawny, young woman posing to show off her arm muscles. The slogan "We Can Do It!" emphasized Rosie's strength. The point of the campaign was to recruit women to work in factories. In other words, women were being asked to do "men's work."

Prior to 1943, tens of thousands of men had flocked to recruiting centers to answer the call to war. Their departure left gaps on the home front. The all-important war industries, companies that made uniforms, weapons, ammunition, ships and planes, for example, lost workers daily as men enlisted or were drafted. At the same time, the factories needed to increase production to meet the war's needs.

American women answered the call. Between 1940 and 1945, six million women joined the workforce. That number is significant, but the types of jobs they were doing is even more noteworthy. Women unloaded freight, operated trains, and used heavy machinery in huge, dirty, noisy factories. Never before had women done those kinds of jobs. An inscription on a bench at the Rosie the Riveter Memorial in Richmond, California, summarizes the importance of these women: "You must tell your children, putting modesty aside, that without us, without women, there would have been no spring in 1945."

Lesson 1 Informational Writing

Here are the features of informational writing:

- It gives important information about a topic.

- It presents a main idea, which is supported with facts.

- It may include information from several different sources.

- It draws a conclusion based on the information presented.

- It is organized in a logical way. Transition words connect ideas.

When writers write to inform, they use transition words to connect ideas. Transition words help readers understand connections among ideas. Here are some common transition words:

again	before long	in spite of
also	but	prior to
and	finally	therefore
as a result	for example	though
at the same time	however	when
because	in addition	

Look back at Cayden's report on page 104. Find the transition words that he used. Circle them.

Now, explore what you could write a report about. It is always a good idea to choose a topic in which you are interested. If you are studying American history and you think military information is boring, don't choose to write about troop movements during 1944. Instead, choose wartime airplane technology or food rationing. To help you think of possible topics, answer these questions.

What places in the world would you like to visit?

_____   _____   _____

_____   _____   _____

What are some historical places, events, or people that you know about? It could be a local historic home or a war memorial.

_____   _____   _____

_____   _____   _____

Lesson 2 Facts, Opinions, and Bias

You already know what facts and opinions are. Facts can be proven to be true. Opinions are judgments that people make based on their beliefs. What about bias?

Bias is an unfair "slant" that a writer gives to a topic. Some writers may do it by accident. Perhaps they have such strong views that they don't realize they are presenting only one point of view or only a portion of the facts. Other writers bias their work on purpose to present their own views and to persuade others to believe as they do.

Can you find the bias—the unfair slant—in this part of a report about the home front during World War II?

Those women who went to work in war factories were more courageous than the men who went into battle. For thousands of years, men have gone to war. Soldiering is an accepted role for a man. Women, however, have always been in charge of the home. During World War II, when women became welders, crane operators, and railroad workers, they changed history. Think of the courage it took to deny thousands of years of training and to take on jobs that no one had ever thought they could even do. These millions of strong women are the "soldiers" who won the war.

The writer clearly feels strongly about the topic. She states her opinion in the first sentence, then supports the topic sentence with other sentences, most of which are opinions. Opinions are fine, but whether these women were braver or more important than the soldiers is a very emotional and arguable point.

How could this writer have avoided bias? In other words, how could she have made her coverage of the topic more fair? Record your ideas here.

_____

_____

_____

_____

_____

_____

_____

_____

Lesson 2 Facts, Opinions, and Bias

As a reader, it is important you to recognize bias when you see it. Advertisements often include bias, which can be a persuasive tool. News stories might contain bias, which could lead you to misunderstand an event or issue. So, it is important to think about what is fact and what is opinion and to ask whether all sides of an issue are being fairly presented. As a writer, you should ask the same questions.

Imagine that you are to write an article about two candidates for class president. One candidate is a girl, and the other candidate is a boy. Make up details so that your report is fair and balanced. Note the strengths of each candidate.

_____

_____

_____

_____

_____

_____

_____

_____

_____

_____

_____

_____

_____

_____

_____

_____

_____

_____

_____

_____

_____

_____

_____

Lesson 3 Reliable Sources

Where do you go when you need information? To the library? To a computer? To a person?

Now, answer this question: Which sources of information are best?

It depends on what you want to know.

Consider the sources listed below. For each question, think about what source would be best, or most useful, based on the type of information required. For some questions, more than one source might be useful. Write the letter of the best source or sources next to each question.

A. atlas	E. online encyclopedia
B. almanac	F. print encyclopedia
C. dictionary	G. topic-specific Web site
D. newspaper	

_____ **1.** What did Rosie the Riveter posters look like?

_____ **2.** Where is the Normandy Coast?

_____ **3.** How many American soldiers died in battle in World War II?

_____ **4.** How many national war memorials are there?

_____ **5.** What towns lie near the border between Poland and Germany?

_____ **6.** Who won last night's soccer match?

_____ **7.** How does the word *Axis* relate to World War II?

Lesson 3 Reliable Sources

Once you find a source that seems to have the information you need, you must decide whether the source is reliable. If the source is printed, ask yourself these questions:

- When was this source published? If you need current information, the book should be only one or two years old. Depending on the subject, even that might be too old.

- **Who wrote this book and for what purpose?** If the book is an encyclopedia, atlas, or almanac, you can be pretty confident that responsible authors wrote it to provide information. If it is a magazine article or a work of nonfiction, you need to ask more questions. Might there be bias in the material? Is the author an expert in the field? Read the book jacket or an "About the Author" blurb to discover as much as you can about the author and the purpose for writing.

If the source is online, there are other questions to ask. Keep in mind that anyone can create a Web site. Just because you see information on a Web site does not mean that it is accurate.

- **What person or organization established or maintains this Web site?** What makes this person or organization an expert on the topic?

- **What is the purpose of the site?** No matter who maintains a site, there is the potential for bias. Does the person or organization want to inform, to sell something, or to present a certain point of view (which may or may not be biased)?

- **When was the site last updated?** Just as with print sources, the publication date may matter, depending on whether you need current information.

Write *yes* or *no* to indicate whether these sources might be reliable, based on the topics given.

_____ You are writing about the Battle of the Bulge. You refer to a 10-year-old book written by soldiers who fought there.

_____ You are writing about D-Day. You refer to an online article written by a person who recently visited the battlefield.

Lesson 4 Taking Notes

When you collect information for a report or presentation, you should take notes. Once you locate a reliable source, your job is first to skim to make sure the source is really what you need. Then, you read carefully. Finally, you paraphrase, or briefly state in your own words, what you have read and record it on note cards or in a writing notebook.

Here is a note card that Cayden wrote when he did his research on Rosie the Riveter.

Cayden knows that one part of his report will be about women in the workforce. He marks each note card with a specific topic. Labeling the cards in this way will make it easier to organize his ideas and write his draft.

Cayden wrote his notes. He recorded important pieces of information.

Women in workforce

1940—12 million
1945—18 million

Production of "durable goods" (war materials)
1940—women were 8% of workforce
1945—women 25% of workforce

www.rosietheriveter.org/faq

Cayden wrote the name of the source. If he needs to go back and check a fact or get more information, he can do it easily.

NAME _____

Lesson 4 Taking Notes

Your assignment is to write a report like Cayden did about America's home front during World War II. Choose a topic such as food rationing, victory gardens, war bonds, or women in the workforce. Then, locate a reliable source and take some notes. Decide how your report will be organized and label each card with one of your main topics. Remember to keep your notes brief and to list your source at the bottom of each card.

Lesson 5 Using an Outline

An **outline** is a way to organize information. If you are writing a report, it is an excellent step to take during the prewriting stage. After you collect information and take notes, you can outline the information to make sure you have everything you need.

Here is the outline Cayden made after he completed his research on Rosie the Riveter.

Rosie the Riveter

I. The Rosie campaign
    A. War Manpower Commission and Office of War Information
    B. Appearance of posters
        1. Attractive
        2. Young
        3. "Brawny"
        4. "We Can Do It!" slogan
    C. Purpose
        1. Recruit women to work in factories
        2. "Men's work"
II. Reason for campaign
    A. Thousands of men had enlisted
    B. No one to fill jobs
    C. War industries
        1. Uniforms
        2. Weapons & ammunition
        3. Ships
        4. Planes
    D. Production increase was needed
III. Women in workforce
    A. Jumped from 12 million to 18 million between 1940–1945
    B. New jobs
        1. Unload freight
        2. Operate trains
        3. Use heavy machinery

Cayden had three "big ideas." Each is designated in the outline with a roman numeral. Under each big idea are topics, labeled with letters. Sometimes, a topic has specific supporting details. Those ideas or facts are labeled with the numbers 1, 2, and so on. Note that information is recorded in short words and phrases. This format is called a **topic outline**. A **sentence outline** would show all entries in complete sentences.

Lesson 5 Using an Outline

Look back at the note cards you created on page 111. Create part of an outline from those notes. Go back to the source if you need additional information. Remember, the format and the labels look like this:

I. Main Idea

    A. Topic

        1. Supporting detail

        2. Supporting detail

_____

_____

_____

_____

_____

_____

_____

_____

_____

_____

_____

_____

_____

_____

_____

_____

_____

_____

_____

_____

_____

_____

Lesson 6 Citing Sources

The last page of a report is a **bibliography**, or an alphabetic list of sources. The bibliography shows readers what sources you used and allows them to consult those sources if they want further information. It also shows your teacher that you used a variety of sources and made good choices.

In a bibliography, you need to give certain specific information so that another person can locate that same source. Each type of source has a slightly different format. Here are examples of bibliographic entries for the most common types of sources. If, for any entry, you don't have a piece of information, skip it and go on to the next piece of information. Pay close attention to punctuation. Periods, commas, quotation marks, and underlining are all part of the format.

Encyclopedia (print or CD-ROM)

Author (if given) last name, first name. "Title of Article." Title of Encyclopedia. Year published. Volume number, Page number.

> "Rosie the Riveter." Microsoft Encarta 96 Encyclopedia. 1996. Volume 18, 112–114.

Book

Author last name, first name. Title of Book. Publisher, date of publication.

> Reid, Constance Bowman, and Clara Marie Allen. Slacks and Calluses: Our Summer in a Bomber Factory. Smithsonian Books, 1999.

Magazine article

Author last name, first name. "Title of Article." Title of Magazine date of magazine: page numbers of article.

Mandel, Elizabeth. "Pioneers of Production: Women Industrial Workers in World War II." Journal of Women's History Summer 2002: 158–161.

Web site

Author last name, first name (if given). "Title of Article or Page." Sponsor of web site. Date of article or last update. Web site address (URL)

> Grant, Katie. "Wartime Memories." Rosie the Riveter Trust. November 14, 2005. www.rosietheriveter.org/memory.htm

NOTE: There is no period at the end of the web site citation.

Lesson 6 Citing Sources

Now, create bibliographic entries of your own. Locate one source of each type. They don't all have to be about the same topic. What's important is that you practice using the format for each type of source.

Encyclopedia

_____

_____

_____

Book

_____

_____

_____

Magazine article

_____

_____

_____

Web site

_____

_____

_____

Lesson 7 Writing about Problems and Solutions

One way to organize a report is to use a problem-solution approach. Not all topics fit this format, but many do. While Cayden studied Rosie the Riveter for his history class, he read about women in the workplace. So, for his next report, he is going to write about women in the workplace. Here is the problem-solution chart he made as part of his prewriting stage.

Problem:
Women face challenges in the workplace that most men do not.

↓

Possible solutions:
1. Childcare—on-site daycare, flex hours to accommodate school schedules, work from home
2. Unequal pay—make women aware of their rights, make laws that require equal pay for men and women
3. Discrimination—enforce non-discrimination laws, empower women to pursue non-traditional jobs

↓

Recommended solution:
Reward companies (possibly with tax breaks) that create nondiscriminatory and equitable workplaces for women.

When Cayden writes his report, he will state the problem, then explore each possible solution. Finally, he will state his recommended solution and give reasons why he thinks it is the best solution to the problem.

Lesson 7 Writing about Problems and Solutions

Think of a topic that interests you. It might be an workplace issue, such as Cayden addressed. Or it could be an issue such as global warming, water quality, or your local landfill. Complete the problem-solution chart on this page.

Problem:

↓

Possible solutions:

↓

Recommended solution:

Lesson 8 The Writing Process: Informational Writing

Students write reports to learn about something or to show what they know. Use the writing process to write a report about a topic that interests you.

Prewrite

Look back at the topic ideas you recorded on page 105. Which one seems most interesting? Choose one and begin to explore that topic with the help of this chart.

Topic: _____

What I Know	What I Want to Know	How or Where I Might Find Out

If you are comfortable with this subject, conduct research and take notes. Remember to organize your note cards by specific topic. For example, Cayden organized his Rosie the Riveter note cards in these categories: The Rosie campaign, the reason for the campaign, and women in the workforce.

Lesson 8 The Writing Process: Informational Writing

Now, it is time to focus on putting ideas in order. Think about your topic. How should you organize the information? By cause and effect, in order of importance, or in problem-solution format? Looking at and organizing your note cards might help you decide. List your main points or ideas in order on this page.

Subject: _____

Method of organization: _____

Lesson 8 The Writing Process: Informational Writing

Draft

Now, write a first draft of your report. Continue on another sheet of paper if you need to. Keep your notes and the chart on page 119 nearby. As you write, don't worry about misspelling words or getting everything perfect. Just write your ideas down in sentences and paragraphs.

_____

_____

_____

_____

_____

_____

_____

_____

_____

_____

_____

_____

_____

_____

_____

_____

_____

_____

_____

_____

_____

_____

_____

_____

_____

Lesson 8 The Writing Process: Informational Writing

Revise

All writers can improve their work. Keep in mind that even experienced writers feel that revising is more difficult than writing the first draft. Read your report as if you are seeing it for the first time. Answer the questions below about your draft. If you answer "no" to any of these questions, those are the areas that might need improvement. Mark your draft so you know what needs more work.

- Did you present information clearly and in a logical order?

- Does each paragraph consist of a main idea supported by facts?

- Did you include transition words to connect ideas?

- Did you begin with a sentence that will make readers want to keep going?

- Did all sentences stay on topic?

- Did you use information from several different sources?

- Did you draw a conclusion based on the information presented?

- Did you keep your audience in mind by asking yourself what they might already know or what they need to know?

- Did you present a fair and balanced view of the subject?

Here are a few pointers about making your report interesting to read.

- Vary the length of your sentences. Mixing short, medium, and long sentences keeps your readers interested.

- Vary the style of your sentences. Begin sentences with different kinds of words or clauses. For example, begin some sentences with verbs, some with phrases (such as "In the airplane factories,..."), and some with clauses (such as "When recruiting women,...").

On page 122, write the revision of your draft. As you revise, pay special attention to the length and style of your sentences.

Lesson 8 The Writing Process: Informational Writing

_____

_____
_____
_____
_____
_____
_____
_____
_____
_____
_____
_____
_____
_____
_____
_____
_____
_____
_____
_____
_____
_____
_____
_____
_____
_____
_____
_____
_____

Lesson 8 The Writing Process: Informational Writing

Proofread

Now is the time to correct those last mistakes. Proofreading is easier if you look for just one kind of error at a time. So, read through once for capital letters. Read again for punctuation, spelling, and so on. Use this checklist as you proofread your report.

____	Each sentence begins with a capital letter.
____	Each sentence states a complete thought.
____	Each sentence is punctuated correctly.
____	All proper nouns begin with capital letters.
____	All words are spelled correctly.

Use standard proofreading symbols as you proofread your revised report.

Remember to read your writing out loud during the proofreading stage. You may hear a mistake or an awkward spot that you did not see.

- <u>c</u>apitalize this letter.
- Add a missing end mark: ⊙ ? !
- Add a comma please.
- Fix incorect or misspelled words.
- Delete this word.
- Lowercase this ℓetter.

Publish

Write or type a final copy of your report on a separate sheet of paper. Write carefully and neatly so that there are no mistakes. Make a cover page for the front and a bibliography for the end. Present your report to the class.

Writer's Handbook

Parts of Speech

A **noun** is a word that names a person, place, or thing. Common nouns name general things. Proper nouns name specific things and always begin with a capital letter.

Common Nouns	Proper Nouns
officer	Sergeant Rhimes
racehorse	Seattle Slew
park	Yellowstone National Park
store	Becker Hardware

A **verb** is an action word. Verbs also show a state of being. Every complete sentence has at least one verb. Verbs show action in the past, in the present, and in the future.

Last week, my team *lost*.
I *was* sad about the loss.
Today, my team *plays* against Sutherland.
Next week, we *will play* at Hinton.

An **adjective** modifies, or describes, a noun or pronoun. Adjectives tell *what kind, how much* or *how many*, or *which one*.

The *brick* building is the Community Center. *(what kind)*
It has *two* entrances. *(how many)*
I usually use *this* entrance. *(which one)*

An **adverb** modifies a verb, an adjective, or another adverb. Adverbs tell *how, when, where*, or *to what degree*.

We planned the parade *carefully*. *(how)*
We chose the date *already*. *(when)*
The parade route will go *there*. *(where)*
We are *completely* prepared. *(to what degree)*

Writer's Handbook

Punctuation

End marks on sentences show whether a sentence is a statement, a command, a question, or an exclamation.

> This sentence makes a statement**.**
> Make your bed, please**.**
> Why might you want to ask a question**?**
> I can't believe how excited you are**!**

Commas help keep ideas clear.

> In a list or series: The parade had floats, bands, and old cars.
> In a compound sentence: I waved at my dad, but I'm not sure he saw me.
> After an introductory phrase or clause: After the parade, we all had ice cream.
> To separate a speech tag: I said to Dad, "Did you see me?"

Quotation marks show the exact words that a speaker says. They enclose the speaker's words and the punctuation that goes with the words.

> "Sure, I saw you," Dad said. "How could I have missed that red hat?"
> "That's exactly why I wore it," I said.

Colons are used to introduce a series, to set off a clause, for emphasis, in time, and in business letter greetings.

> My favorite vegetables include the following: *broccoli, red peppers, and spinach.* *(series)*

> The radio announcer said: *"The game is postponed due to rain."* *(clause)*

> The skiers expected the worst as they got off the mountain: *an avalanche.* *(emphasis)*

Writer's Handbook

The Writing Process

When writers write, they take certain steps. Those steps make up the writing process.

Step 1: Prewrite

First, writers choose a topic. Then, they collect and organize ideas or information. They might write their ideas in a list. They might also make a chart and begin to put their ideas in some kind of order.

Tomika is going to write about her dance lessons. She put her ideas in a web.

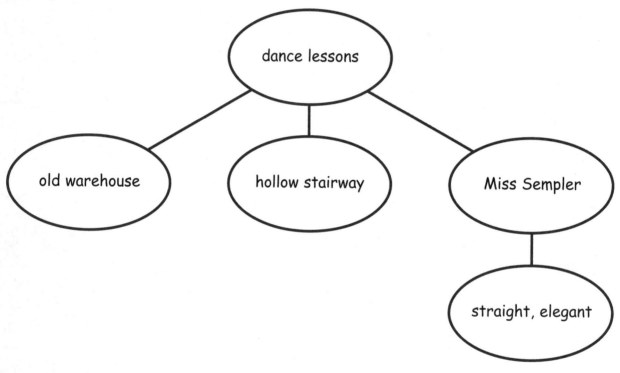

Step 2: Draft

Next, writers put their ideas on paper in a first draft. Writers know that there might be mistakes in this first draft. That's okay. Here is Tomika's first draft.

> Every Wednesday after school I eagerly climb the hollow stairway of the old Benson's Warehouse building I am glad to go dance lessons, even if they are in an old warehouse. Miss Sempler always greets the other students and me. She is so straight and elagant. She says we sound like a heard of hippoes coming up the stairs. I try to go up the stairs with my head high and my shoulders back, just like miss Sempler would.

Writer's Handbook

Step 3: Revise

Then, writers change or fix their first draft. They might decide to move ideas around or to add information. They might also take out words or sentences that don't belong. Here are Tomika's changes.

> Every Wednesday after school I eagerly climb the hollow, *echoing* stairway of the old Benson's Warehouse building I am glad to go *to* dance lessons, even if they are in an old warehouse. Miss Sempler always greets the other students and me. *at the top of the stairs* She is so straight and elagant. She says we sound like a heard of hippoes coming up the stairs. I try to go up the stairs with my head high and my shoulders back, just like miss Sempler would. *I almost feel like a dancer even before I get to class.*

Step 4: Proofread

Writers usually write a new copy so their writing is neat. Then, they read again to make sure everything is correct. They read for mistakes in their sentences. Tomika found several more mistakes when she proofread her work.

> Every Wednesday after school, I eagerly climb the hollow, echoing stairway of the old Benson's Warehouse building, I am glad to go to dance lessons, even if they are in an old warehouse. Miss Sempler always greets the other students and me at the top of the stairs. She is so straight and elagant. She says we sound like a heard of hippoes coming up the stairs. I try to go up the stairs with my head high and my shoulders back, just like miss Sempler would. I almost feel like a dancer even before I get to class.

Step 5: Publish

Finally, writers make a final copy that has no mistakes. They are now ready to share their writing with a reader. They might choose to read their writing out loud. They can also add pictures and create a book. There are many ways for writers to publish, or to share, their work with readers.

Writer's Handbook

Personal Narrative

In a personal narrative, a writer writes about something he has done or seen. A personal narrative can be about anything, as long as the writer is telling about one of his or her own experiences. Here is the final version of Tomika's paragraph about dance lessons.

Words that tell time indicate when something happens.	The words *I* and *me* show that the writer is part of the action.

Every Wednesday after school, I eagerly climb the hollow, echoing stairway of the old Benson's Warehouse building. I am glad to go to dance lessons, even if they are in an old warehouse. Miss Sempler always greets the other students and me at the top of the stairs. She is so straight and elegant. She says we sound like a herd of hippos coming up the stairs. I try to go up the stairs with my head high and my shoulders back, just like Miss Sempler would. I almost feel like a dancer even before I get to class.

Describing words and figurative language help readers "see" or "hear" what is happening.	The writer stayed on topic. All of the sentences give information about Tomika's dance lesson.

Descriptive Writing

When writers describe, they might tell about an object, a place, or an event. They use sensory words so that readers can see, hear, smell, feel, or taste whatever is being described. In this example of descriptive writing, Brad described the results of his science experiment.

The writer uses the whole-to-whole comparison method. He describes one plant in this paragraph, and the other plant in the next paragraph.	Sensory details help readers visualize the scene.

Daisy plant A was my control plant. It received the same amount of water as plant B, but it received no Epsom salts. Plant A has 9 leaves and is 12.5 inches tall. Its leaves are bright green, and it has a healthy appearance.

Daisy plant B received two doses of Epsom salts. The first dose was administered just as the first leaves appeared, and the second was administered one week later. Plant B has 14 leaves and is 14 inches tall. This plant also has 2 flower buds. The leaves are a deep green, and the plant is fuller and has a more pleasing appearance than does daisy plant A.

The writer gives information in the same order in each paragraph.

Writer's Handbook

Fiction Stories

Writers write about made-up things. They might write about people or animals. The story might seem real, or it might seem unreal, or fantastic. Here is a story that Jason wrote. It has human characters, and the events could really happen, so Jason's story is realistic.

The story has a beginning, a middle, and an end.

This story is written in third-person point of view. The narrator is not a part of the action. So, words such as *he, she, her, him,* and *they* refer to the characters.

Bitter Victory

Coach had put Neil out on the field. He hadn't played all season. Neil suspected that Coach felt sorry for him, but he was glad to be in the game. Not that he figured anything would actually happen. But then, there was the ball. A Hampton player had fumbled it, and fumbled it badly. It was skittering crazily across the chewed-up grass. Now, it was coming right at him.

Neil picked up the ball and looked frantically all around him. There was a lot of confusion. Without his realizing it, Neil's feet were moving. No one was taking much notice. He crouched down a little to hide the ball tucked under his arm. He made his feet go faster and headed for the end zone. He gritted his teeth, expecting to get clobbered. Forty…thirty…twenty…ten…*Whumpf*!

A Hampton player caught him at the last moment. The impact sent Neil careening forward. He stumbled over the line, completely out of control. A sting in his ankle was quickly forgotten; Neil tasted dirt and grass as he rolled and finally came to a stop. Grinning at his approaching teammates, Neil yelled, "We won! We won!"

Neil's teammates were all yelling at him, but not about winning the game. Neil looked down at his ankle, which was bent at a nauseating angle. A blur of noises and movements occurred as Neil was loaded onto a stretcher and carried off. What he remembered, though, was the scoreboard, and the fact that the crowd went wild, just like in the movies.

The first paragraph establishes the setting.

Sensory words help readers visualize what is happening.

Time and order words keep ideas clear.

Informational Writing

When writers write to inform, they present information about a topic. Informational writing is nonfiction. It is not made up; it contains facts.

Here is a paragraph from a report about the Olympics.

The writer states the main idea in a topic sentence. It is the first sentence of the paragraph.

The Olympics

The tradition of the Olympics is a long and honorable one. The first Olympics were played in Greece more than 2,500 years ago. The initial contest was held in 776 B.C. There was just one event—a footrace. Later, the Greeks added boxing, wrestling, chariot racing, and the pentathlon. The ancient Games were held every four years for more than a thousand years.

These sentences contain details that support the main idea.

A time-order word connects ideas.

Writer's Handbook

Explanatory (or How-to) Writing

When writers explain how to do things, they might tell how to make a craft, play a computer game, or use a cell phone. Tony has written instructions for Jenna, who is going to take care of Tony's hamster while he is on vacation.

The first sentence summarizes the care instructions.

Order words help readers keep the steps in order.

Each day when you come, there are three things to do. First, check Heidi's water to make sure the bottle hasn't fallen out of place. Then fill her food dish. Her food is in the green bag next to the cage. Finally, play with Heidi. She would love to snuggle in your neck and maybe crawl down your sleeve.

Clear words help readers understand the instructions.

Persuasive Writing

In persuasive writing, writers try to make readers think, feel, or act in a certain way. Persuasive writing shows up in newspaper and magazine articles, letters to the editor, business letters, and, of course, advertisements. Trina has written a letter to the editor of her school newsletter.

The writer begins by stating her opinion.

The writer uses an emotional appeal to persuade readers to agree with her.

Dear Editor:
    The locker bay is a mess. So many of the lockers are old, scratched, and dented. Some of them don't even close properly. How can we be proud of our school when the locker room is falling apart? More importantly, the worn-out lockers seem to encourage students to mistreat them even further. Someone needs to repair or replace the lockers so that we can feel good about our school.
Trina Hardesty

The writer states facts to lend support to her opinions.

The writer includes a specific request for action.

Writer's Handbook

Business Letters

Writers write business letters to people or organizations with whom they are not familiar. Business letters usually involve a complaint or a request for information. Mariko needs information for a school report. She wrote a business letter to request information.

The heading includes the sender's address and the date.

8213 Rivera Boulevard
Fredericksburg, TX 78624
March 4, 2008

The inside address is the complete name and address of the recipient.

Dr. Olivia Lamas, DVM
Lamas Animal Clinic
944 Curry Lane
Fredericksburg, TX 78624

Dear Dr. Lamas:

A colon follows the greeting.

My class is exploring careers this month. I would like to learn about being a veterinarian. Is there a time when I can visit your office? I have many questions, and I would like to watch you work with the animals.

The text of the letter is the body.

Please call my teacher, Ms. Zapata, to set up a time that is convenient for you. The school's phone number is 830-555-0021.

Thank you for your help, and I look forward to meeting you.

Sincerely,

A comma follows the closing.

Mariko Campillo
Mariko Campillo

The sender always includes a signature.

Answer Key

Chapter 1

Lesson 1

Page 5
Underlined topic sentence: I think city life is great.
Crossed-out sentence: We usually ride the 9:15 express when we go across town to visit my grandma.
Paragraphs will vary.

Lesson 2

Page 7
Order of steps shown:
Step 5: Publish
Step 3: Revise
Step 4: Proofread
Step 1: Prewrite
Step 2: Draft

Lesson 3

Page 8
The writer failed to provide an explanation of what shirred eggs are and how to prepare them.

Page 9
Memos will vary.

Lesson 4

Page 10
Details will vary.
Paragraphs will vary.

Page 11
Revised, proofread, and rewritten paragraphs will vary.

Chapter 2

Lesson 1

Page 14
Responses to idea-starters will vary.

Lesson 2

Page 15
Time words and phrases will vary.
Sentences will vary.

Page 16
Circled words in paragraph: *When, finally, as, At last*
Paragraphs will vary.

Lesson 3

Page 18
Students should notice that the paragraph that uses passive voice is longer than the paragraph that uses active voice.
Andy Hunley hit a home run.
The crowd was cheering
X The last run was scored by Gabe Cruz.
X The game was won by the Warriors.
Sentences will vary.

Lesson 4

Page 19
Ideas and idea webs will vary.

Page 20
Entries in sequence charts will vary.

Page 21
Sensory details will vary.

Page 22
Drafts will vary.

Page 24
Revisions will vary.

Answer Key

Chapter 3

Lesson 1

Page 26
Possible details:
See: century-old, colorful fish, wall-sized aquarium, gleaming golden oak tables..., red flocked wallpaper
Hear: smacking your lips
Smell: meats, seasoned potatoes, fresh vegetables
Touch: gleaming golden oak tables and chairs, red flocked wallpaper
Taste: perfectly prepared meats, interestingly seasoned potatoes, crisp-tender fresh vegetables
Details will vary.

Page 27
Details and paragraphs will vary.

Lesson 2

Page 28
Possible revised sentences:
One nervous singer performed a shaky solo.
The girls wore long blue dresses.
The boys wore black pants and white shirts.
The young director bowed to the cheering audience.

Page 29
Possible revised sentences:
One singer nervously performed a solo.
He nearly dropped the microphone once.
The judges clapped and nodded their heads encouragingly.
The audience stood immediately and clapped for the happy soloist.
The soloist's grateful mother quietly wiped tears from her eyes.
The relieved singer left the stage quickly.

The tired director went home happily and rested his aching feet.

Lesson 3

Page 30
Spatial words: *left, in, Beyond, right, next, far, side*

Page 31
Descriptive paragraphs will vary.

Lesson 4

Page 32
Details and paragraphs will vary.

Page 33
Details and paragraphs will vary.

Lesson 5

Page 34
Comparative sentences will vary.
Comparative forms used should be *more appealing, heavier, taller, yellower*.

Page 35
Comparative sentences will vary.
Comparative forms used should be *darkest, smoothest, tiniest, most unusual*.

Lesson 6

Page 36
Entries in Venn diagrams will vary.

Page 37
Paragraphs will vary.

Lesson 7

Page 38
Entries in Venn diagrams will vary.

Page 39
Comparisons will vary.

Answer Key

Chapter 3 continued

Lesson 8

Page 40
Possible similes:
The flowers were as blue as the sky.
My wet shoes seemed as heavy as lead.
The tree outside my window glows yellow
   like the sun.
The flower's petals fluttered in the wind
   like a butterfly's wings.
Descriptions and similes will vary.

Page 41
a lantern and the moon
Possible metaphors:
The baby's hand was a feather on my
   palm.
The rainbow was a snake arching across
   the sky.
Descriptions and metaphors will vary.

Lesson 9

Page 42
Topic ideas will vary.
Entries in idea webs will vary.

Page 43
Methods of organization and paragraphs
   will vary.

Page 44
Revisions will vary.

Page 45
Published descriptive paragraphs will vary.

Chapter 4

Lesson 1

Page 48
Narrator: a third-person narrator, not a
   character in the story
Main character: Kler
Possible details: She milks a herd of
   tambles, has an older brother, has two
   parents, lives near Tarboon
Learn about character: through narrator
Other characters: Father, Mother, Fron
Learn about other characters: through
   narrator
Setting: in a barn
Setting details: sky glows green, ground is
   dusty, broad-leaved flanda plants
   "glow," dim barn, pipes in milking room
Possible problem: There might be a
   conflict with the Chief in Tarboon; there
   might be a problem with Fron's quest.
Dialogue (possible answers): She seems to
   like the animals.
Sensory details: green glowing sky, dusty
   dirt, warm nest, warm, earthy barn, high-
   pitched bleats, playful nips, rubbery lips,
   long necks, furry, three-toed beasts, milk
   whirred and swished, ticking of a clock,
   CLANK-CLANK, scraping noise, darkest
   corner, prickle, gut-wrenching blow,
   black eyes, pale face

Lesson 2

Page 49
Possible details and senses:
sky glowed green—sight
barn—sight
dusty ground—sight, touch
broad leaves shimmer, glow—sight
warm nest—sight, touch
stir, cook, bottle—sight, touch, smell

Answer Key

Page 50
Information from passage: caves, dragons live in them, an old volcano looms nearby
Mood or feeling (possible responses): The mood is somewhat serious, maybe a little mysterious.
Responses will vary.

Page 51
Responses and paragraphs will vary.

Lesson 3

Page 52
Characters listed will vary.
"Kler's Quest" character details (possible answers):
Character is a female—the narrator uses *she*, etc.
Character sleeps in a nest—narrator reveals information
Character has a brother and mother and father—narrator reveals information
Character likes tambles—narrator reveals that she smiles about them

Page 53
Responses and paragraphs will vary.

Lesson 4

Page 54
Learn about Kler from dialogue (possible responses): She respects her father. She is curious.
Learn about Father from dialogue: He is concerned about Fron. He is used to being obeyed by his children. He is surprised by the situation.

Page 55
"Why shouldn't I speak of it?" Kler asked.
Father replied, "No one must know."
"What about," Kler continued, "the Chief in Tarboon?"

"Absolutely no one," replied Father.
Dialogue will vary.

Lesson 5

Page 57
Rewritten paragraph:
    I hadn't minded the job, at first. My older brother, who used to do the milking, was gone on his quest. He hadn't wanted to go, but Father had made him. The Chief in Tarboon said it was time. Father didn't want to attract attention, so, with what I thought was deep regret, Father had sent Fron away.
Paragraphs will vary.

Lesson 6

Page 58
Responses will vary.
Realistic story ideas will vary.

Page 59
Responses will vary.
Fantasy story ideas will vary.

Lesson 7

Page 60
Story maps will vary.

Page 61
Character details in idea webs will vary.
Setting details will vary.

Page 62
Entries in sequence charts will vary.

Page 63
Drafts will vary.

Page 65
Revisions will vary.

Page 67
Final versions will vary.

Answer Key

Chapter 5

Lesson 1

Page 68

The writer tells readers to talk to their city representatives to make their wishes known.

Page 69

Persuasive articles will vary.

Lesson 2

Page 70

Circled opinion signal words: *should, believe, should, best, should, must*

Page 71

Possible facts from article on page 70:

Daily traffic on East Morgan Avenue has increased....; That part of town's population has increased.; City planners want to expand the road.; The road is the main east-west artery through the city.

Possible opinions from article on page 70:

Area traffic is congested.; Taxpayers should support road expansion.; It is in the best interests of the city to expand road.; People should vote "yes."

Fact from Mr. Lewis's e-mail:

Road expansion would put road up against the storefronts.

Circled opinion signal words: *think, never, worst, believe*

Possible opinions from Mr. Lewis's paragraph:

Road expansion is "nuts."; Buildings will not be able to handle stress.; This is the city planners' worst idea.; Road expansion would ruin neighborhood.

Students' personal opinions will vary.

Lesson 3

Page 72

Issues will vary.

Page 73

The emotional appeal in Mr. Alvarez's letter is aimed at strong feelings that people have about progress and being "modern." In essence, he accuses Ms. Marple of being old-fashioned or of getting in the way or progress.

Letters to the editor will vary.

Page 74

Possible response: The ad sends the message that if you eat at the diner, you will be happy. It also appeals to people's desire to feel good about themselves and to satisfy themselves (with good food).

Slogans and advertisements will vary.

Lesson 4

Page 75

Reasons why the school should not adjust the school day:

1) Some school bus routes would begin as early as 6 a.m.

2) Research shows that teenagers' bodies need more sleep.

3) Getting up at 5 a.m. will not benefit 13- to 19-year-olds.

4) The new schedule would release these same children at 2:30 p.m.

5) That means a whole extra hour for many children to be on their own before parents get home from work.

6) <u>In many families, parents depart for work and leave older children responsible for younger children. If older children get on the bus an hour earlier, some younger children may be left unsupervised.</u>

Page 76
Prewriting notes and letters will vary.

Lesson 5
Page 78
Letters of request will vary, but should follow standard business letter format.

Page 79
Letters of complaint will vary, but should follow standard business letter format.

Lesson 6
Page 80
Students' ideas will vary.
Entries in idea webs will vary.

Page 81
Students' organizational notes will vary.

Page 82
Drafts will vary.

Page 84
Revisions will vary.

Chapter 6

Lesson 1
Page 86
Responses will vary.

Page 87
Order words underlined in paragraph: *First, Then, Next, Finally*
Responses will vary.

Lesson 2
Page 88
Circled cause-and-effect words in paragraph: *caused, so, As a result, because*
Possible causes and effects:
Cause: Plenty of rainfall. Effect: Land produced well.
Cause: Drought. Effect: Land did not produce well.
Cause: Crops failed. Effect: There was no vegetation to hold soil in place.
Cause: Soil is bare and dry. Effect: Dust clouds arise when wind blows.

Page 89
Possible causes and effects:
Cause: Charlotte's father arranges for her voyage. Effect: Charlotte sails to America.
Cause: Charlotte's father owns the ship. Effect: Everyone thinks Charlotte will be safe.
Cause: Ship's captain has a good reputation. Effect: Everyone thinks Charlotte will be safe.
Cause: Traveling companions do not show up. Effect: Charlotte is alone on the voyage.
Responses will vary.

Answer Key

Page 90
Responses will vary.

Page 91
Responses will vary.

Lesson 3

Page 92
Circled words in paragraph: *so, so, Because, As a result, resulted*
Possible causes and effects:
Cause: Election is a month away. Effect: A "Meet the Candidates" night was held.
Cause: A "Meet the Candidates" night was held. Effect: Several hundred people attended.
Cause: The race for state representative is hotly contested . Effect: Many people were eager to hear those two candidates.
Cause: Tincher became ill. Effect: He was unable to attend.
Cause: Tincher became ill and was unable to attend. Effect: Kimura suggested that he could not do his job well.

Page 93
Responses will vary.
Paragraphs will vary.

Lesson 4

Page 95
Visual aids will vary.

Lesson 5

Page 96
Underlined words in paragraph: *First, Then, to east, left, two blocks, right, over, past, right*

Page 97
Directions will vary.

Lesson 6

Page 98
Responses and entries in idea webs will vary.

Page 99
Entries in organizational chart will vary.

Page 100
First drafts of instructions will vary.

Page 102
Revisions will vary.

Answer Key

Chapter 7

Lesson 1

Page 104
Circled transition words (instructions on page 105): *and, yet, Prior, and, At the same time, Between, but, and, Never before*

Page 105
Topic explorations will vary.

Lesson 2

Page 106
Responses will vary.; The writer could have could have praised the efforts of the women workers without decreasing the importance of men's roles in the war.

Page 107
Articles will vary.

Lesson 3

Page 108
Possible answers:
1. E, F, G
2. A, E, F
3. B, E, F, G
4. B, E
5. A
6. D
7. C,E,F

Page 109
yes
no

Lesson 4

Page 111
Entries on note cards will vary.

Lesson 5

Page 113
Outlines will vary.

Lesson 6

Page 115
Bibliographic entries will vary, but must follow the formats given.

Lesson 7

Page 117
Entries in problem-solution chart will vary.

Lesson 8

Page 118
Entries in K-W-L chart will vary.

Page 119
Entries in organizational chart will vary.

Page 120
Drafts will vary.

Page 122
Revisions will vary.

Notes

Notes

Notes

Notes

Notes